A HISTORY OF
OCEAN
LINERS
IN 50 OBJECTS

A HISTORY OF
OCEAN LINERS
IN 50 OBJECTS

MARK BERRY

All of the objects in this book are from Mark Berry's collection, unless otherwise stated.

First published 2020

The History Press
97 St George's Place, Cheltenham,
Gloucestershire, GL50 3QB
www.thehistorypress.co.uk

British Library Cataloguing in Publication Data.
A catalogue record for this book is available from the British Library.

ISBN 978 0 7509 9432 3

Typesetting and origination by The History Press
Printed in Turkey by Imak

CONTENTS

INTRODUCTION

WHAT IS AN OCEAN LINER?

The definition of an ocean liner is a vessel that runs on a set route to timetable between two or more ports, normally returning to the start point to resume the cycle. A cruise ship is a totally different entity, transporting passengers on a journey that may call at several destinations and which does not generally run to a regular recurring schedule. In this book, you will find that there are occasions where an ocean liner is also used for cruising, but the reverse is rarely the case.

So why is a liner so different? She doesn't generally potter around ports in sunny climes, of course, but she sometimes might do so. Occasionally she might steam up and down fjords, allowing well-nourished passengers to take in stops ashore and to admire stunning scenery between excellent meals and copious amounts of reasonably priced beverages. However, these are diversions;

she was designed and built for a purpose, to keep a schedule, to run line voyages.

Three words sum up the elements of a liner: power, design ... and soul!

From the earliest days of ocean travel, the transport of goods was (apart from war, of course) the prime reason for crossing the oceans. As global transport became more vital to trading nations, the movement of commodities and goods from producers to consumers became of paramount importance. Commercial entities such as the East India Company and the Hanseatic League built or purchased fleets of sailing ships to move goods around Europe and the world. As empires grew, personnel and materials also had to travel around the globe, and as with any commercial enterprise, time was, and still is, money.

The tea clipper races from China to Britain in the 1860s showed how commercial advantage could drive the need for speed at sea. Ships such as *Ariel* and *Taeping* vied to be the first home over a 14,000-mile voyage, rounding the Cape of Good Hope and up through Biscay. *Cutty Sark* was late to the party in the 1870s, but she survives today. If you visit her at Greenwich, it is evident that she is the result, and indeed the personification, of the evolution of the sailing ship from a humble cargo carrier to a finely tuned commercial racing machine. We will return to this concept as applied to the ocean liner later in this book.

POWER

A liner needs to keep a schedule. The business or leisure traveller of today needs to be able to consult a timetable; board a train, ship or aeroplane; and know that there is a good chance that it will leave on time and arrive as expected. In the nineteenth and early twentieth centuries, voyage by sea was the only option for transcontinental travel, and the oceans paid little heed to the certainties of a timetable. When your vessel relied on sail or at best an early and inefficient steam engine, possibly linked to paddle wheels, there was no certainty of keeping to any kind of schedule, if indeed you arrived at your destination at all. It was not unheard of for a nineteenth-century liner to disappear without trace and, as we shall see, it was still quite possible for this to happen to a large, almost new steam-powered liner in the early twentieth century. Power increased as technology advanced, the Parsons steam turbine taking efficiency to a new level after the steam expansion engines that were fitted to most ships in the nineteenth and early twentieth centuries. Turbo electric, diesel engines and gas turbines have all been part of liner evolution. Coal gave way to oil and now concern for the environment pushes forward the development of greener power plants using liquefied natural gas (LNG).

DESIGN

From the earliest designs for ocean liners, it became evident that a streamlined hull with a keel for stability was essential. Crossing the Atlantic, for instance, can often put a ship in conflict with extreme weather and sea conditions. She needs to keep moving ahead, the luxury of running to a sheltered bay or port to ride out bad weather is not an option. She needs good sea-keeping abilities and the strength to cut through or forge over swells and troughs, and sometimes take on extreme waves and hurricane-force winds without damage or risk to life. Early twentieth-century liners such as *Mauretania* had a length to width ratio of around 9:1 and knife-like prows to cut through most sea conditions. Granted they tended to roll, but this was more an inconvenience to passengers than an impediment to progress. New hull designs were tried and led to the revolutionary Vladimir Yourkevitch design for the *Normandie*. Aids to stability developed, both gyro and extending stabilisers. A modern slab-sided cruise ship with a relatively flat bottom is not suited to speed in rough weather, or to having to keep a schedule week after week on long back-to-back crossings in all conditions.

SOUL

Yes, ships do have a soul and none more so than the ocean liner. She is not just a conveyance for passengers but also a home to her crew, who may have spent most of their careers on the same ship. The way the ships were designed and fitted gave individuality. The words luxury and ocean liner are synonymous, but the luxury did not necessarily extend to second- and certainly not to third-class accommodations. Each ship, however, had its own personality. The *Mauretania*, or 'Maury' to her crew, was built on the Tyne and had an interior style using a variety of darker woods, especially mahogany, which gave her more of a traditional feel, akin to a country house at sea. Her sister, *Lusitania* or 'Lusi', was built on the Clyde, had a different designer, James Miller, and had a lighter interior with extensive use of painted plaster. Ostensibly very similar ships but with very different personalities, and to their crews and those passengers who knew them, both had an individuality and a soul.

Some liners were known as 'Happy Ships', with a content, cohesive crew and passengers. A ship that attracted both to sail on her time and again or to stay with her, for some undefined reason. Other ships were less happy and might have a reputation for breaking down, accidents, or just not feel 'right'. The word 'jinxed' could even be applied, though often with hindsight after a mishap or even loss … 'I always said she was a wrong 'un!'

A liner is conceived on the drawing board; birthed on the slipway; and enjoys the exuberance of youth as she takes her place on the seas, maybe breaking records for speed or receiving accolades for her luxury. She reaches middle age, the wrinkles, aches and pains appear, and she starts to struggle to compete with the newer generation of ships. If she is allowed, she will grow old, often attracting love and loyalty from those who have known her. RMS *Olympic* was in service from 1911–35 and became known affectionately as 'Old Reliable'. *Aquitania* sailed from 1914 to 1949, serving in both wars as both hospital and troopship. To those who knew them, these liners and their like had a soul, a life, and were loved, mourned and remembered.

The end, when it came, could be through accident or disaster, or the ship might become uneconomical and outmoded and end her days on the breaking grounds of Scotland, or more recently, run onto the beaches of Bangladesh, India and Pakistan for dismantling. In a very few cases, she would be sold and reborn into a new life. The liner *Stockholm* (1946), which collided with the gorgeous Italian liner *Andrea Doria* in 1956, leading to the latter sinking with the loss of forty-six lives, was still in service in 2020 as the cruise ship *Astoria* with CMV. The great Cunarder *Queen Mary* (1936) is preserved at Long Beach, California, as a museum, hotel and major tourist attraction. These are very much the exceptions, most of the great liners are now gone.

These ships leave their legacy, however, through the memory of passengers, crew, and builders; through anecdote; and, of course, through the objects that remain from their lives in service. From these we can examine these amazing ships and relive their triumphs, as well as the more routine yet no less fascinating aspects of their operation. We can also learn about the people who served on them, enjoyed them as passengers, or sailed aboard on their way to and from war. There are celebrities and emigrants, tourists, evacuees, war brides and babies. We will learn of privilege and poverty, hope and misfortune, triumph and disaster.

Only one true member of the breed still sails. *Queen Mary 2*, which entered service for Cunard in 2004, is an ocean liner in every sense of the word. She runs a regular transatlantic service between Southampton and New York. She also cruises, and both roles she fulfils to an exemplary standard. She was designed by naval architect Stephen Payne OBE and the prime directive was the ability to complete regular Atlantic liner crossings in all seasons. She has a liner hull that is strong and hydrodynamic, with marine diesel engines together with gas turbines driving electric generators linked to four electric motors housed in directional Azipod thrusters under the hull. A far cry from early steam engines and even the Parsons turbine, but I hope that this book will show the link between the present and the past.

How do you chart the history of ocean liners in fifty objects?

This recurring thought has been on my mind since I decided to produce this book. There are maritime historians, cruise lovers, memorabilia collectors and armchair travellers. Some people may pick up this book and wonder, why all the fuss about ocean liners anyway? They are just big ships that go here and there and sometimes sink, they will think, and put the book back where it came from. Others I hope may just be inspired by it to want to learn more.

The book is divided into two halves, the first being objects relating to specific ships, and the second exploring different aspects of the sea journey. One thing is certain: my choice of objects will not satisfy everyone, but being a glass half full kind of author, I hope that you will at least find the voyage worth taking, discover new things and hopefully enjoy some of the on-board entertainment.

Mark Berry
2020

Detail from an RMS *Aquitania* menu of 1948.

RMS *OCEANIC*, ORIGINAL PEN AND INK DRAWING

GREAT BRITAIN, 1899

Oceanic was a revolutionary liner, in that she marked the beginning of a focus for the White Star Line on luxury and comfort over speed. This ethos would culminate in the Olympic-class liners of 1911. *Oceanic* was a one-off, there were no sister ships, although one had been planned. Built at Harland and Wolff, at over 17,000 tons, she was 704 × 68ft and powered by two triple expansion reciprocating steam engines. As usual, first-class accommodation was lavish for the 410 passengers who could afford it. The 1,300 people in second and third class enjoyed less salubrious but nevertheless comfortable facilities for the time.

She joined the Liverpool–New York service, making her maiden voyage on 6 September that year, crossing in six days, two hours thirty-seven minutes. She would subsequently transfer to the Southampton–New York run.

Original pen and ink drawing of RMS *Oceanic*.

Charles Lightoller, the surviving second officer on *Titanic*, had served on *Oceanic* for seven years, joining as third officer and rising to first. He commented on her luxury in his memoirs. The magnificent smoke room doors cost over £500, and there were eighteen carat gold-plated light fittings. In addition, there was a lot of hand-carved wood and specially commissioned art work. The first-class dining room featured a huge glass dome giving natural light and a feeling of space, while the smoke room had a huge mahogany frieze and two domes over.

Oceanic's career was successful, and she gained quite a following among travellers, as often happened with a well-run, well-appointed liner. There was a collision with a much smaller steamer off Ireland in August 1901, which killed seven, but beyond this there were the usual mishaps and damage that could occur crossing the Atlantic in all seasons.

Oceanic was moored at Southampton on the morning of 10 April 1912. Outboard of her to starboard was the liner *New York*. Suction from the departing *Titanic* pulled *New York* entirely adrift and a collision between the ships was narrowly averted. *Oceanic* was partially pulled away from the dock and, according to Lightoller who was on *Titanic*, a 60ft gangway dropped into the water.

On the outbreak of war in 1914, RMS *Oceanic* became HMS *Oceanic* of the Royal Navy as an armed merchant cruiser. Lightoller was back on board as first officer and he became a navy lieutenant with the ships' transfer to the Navy. HMS *Oceanic* now had two captains (never a good idea), RN Captain William Slater and Captain Henry Smith, her normal commander. Patrolling the waters around the Shetlands, for which her size made her totally unsuited, she ran aground on the island of Foula on 8 September 1914. Sitting high and intact on the reef, she was completely consumed during a storm two weeks later and by the following morning she had vanished.

The main image is an original pen and ink drawing by Richard Quiller Lane (1848–1902). He was a Belfast artist who drew for technical publications such as *Engineering Magazine* and *The Shipbuilder*, as well as contemporary postcards. Dated 1899, it shows the liner leaving Belfast for the first time.

Overleaf: RMS *Oceanic* menu, 26 January 1914.

WHITE STAR
LINE

R.M.S. "OCEANIC"

MENU.

Oysters on Half-Shell
Hors-d'œuvre variés

Consommé Monte Carlo   Potage Marigny

Broiled Bluefish, American
COLLARETTE POTATOES

Filet Mignon, Mexicaine

Vol-au-Vent à la Chambord

Globe Artichokes, Barigoule

Roast Ribs & Sirloin of Beef
HORSERADISH

Roast Turkey Poult, Sausage
CRANBERRY SAUCE

Braised Virginia Ham, Roederer

Cauliflower au Gratin   White Squash
Patna Rice
Browned, Boiled, & Pont Neuf Potatoes

Pheasant, Perigod Sauce

Salad Endive

Pouding d'Orleans
Macédoine of Fruit   Pâtisserie Parisienne
Lemon Ice Cream

JANUARY 26TH, 1914

2

SS *WARATAH*, CARD POSTED AT SEA

GREAT BRITAIN, 1908

Waratah still missing. Further list of passengers bound for London. The East Coast from Durban Southwards is still being vigorously searched for any trace of the missing liner Waratah.

London Evening Standard, Wednesday, 18 August 1909

A modern ocean liner, steam powered, brand new, vanishes without trace between Durban and Cape Town in July 1909. SS *Waratah* was launched on 12 September 1908 at the Barclay Curle shipyard on the Clyde. Her owners, Lund's Blue Anchor Line, operated services between London Tilbury and Australian ports, via Las Palmas, Cape Town and Durban. Their business was based on the emigrant trade

SS *Waratah* postcard from maiden voyage.

Lund's Blue Anchor Line officer's cap badge.

to Australia, with the ability to then adapt the ship's carrying capacity to cargo and refrigerated goods for the return journey.

The ship was 465 × 59ft and 9,339 GRT. Power came from two coal-fired quadruple-expansion steam engines driving two screws. Her service speed was around 13 knots. In addition to 300 third-class passengers and up to 700 emigrants in dormitory accommodation (this space could be converted to cargo), she had cabins and staterooms for 128 first-class passengers. There was a children's nursery and the ship had a fresh water distillation plan, but no wireless. The crew numbered 154.

Waratah, named after the state flower of New South Wales, was not a pretty ship. Tall and looking rather top heavy, there was discussion after her loss as to whether she was unstable. She was, however, certified 100 per cent A1 by Lloyd's surveyors on 4 November 1908. Some passengers and crew raised concerns, having been on her maiden voyage, that she rolled and was slow to recover, even having a permanent list. Others felt no such concerns.

She started her maiden voyage, leaving Tilbury for Adelaide, on 5 November 1908, returning on 7 March 1909. Her commander, Captain Joshua Ilbery, was a highly experienced mariner, and her officers and crew competent.

Her last outward voyage began on 27 April 1909, reached Adelaide on 2 July, and then moved on to Melbourne and Sydney to unload and load cargo including bullion, wool and frozen goods. Returning to Adelaide, she embarked eighty-two passengers, as well as refrigerated cargo, butter, grain and lead concentrates. Leaving Adelaide on 7 July, she crossed the Indian Ocean, reaching Durban on the 25th. Here some passengers disembarked and one, engineer Claude Sawyer, left her unexpectedly, citing a series of bad dreams that left him in fear of his life if he continued the voyage aboard *Waratah*. He cabled his wife to say he thought the ship 'top heavy'.

When *Waratah* left Durban for Cape Town on the evening of 26 July, she sailed into history. The last definite sighting of her was by the Clan Line's *Clan Macintyre* at 0600 on the 27th, exchanging signals before *Waratah* overtook her and disappeared into deteriorating weather. Apart from one possible sighting by the Union Castle liner *Guelph* on the evening of the 29th, the *Waratah*, her passengers and crew was never seen or heard from again.

The postcard was sent from the *Waratah* on her maiden voyage, and indicates a pleasant voyage with no hint of any problems.

3

RMS *LUSITANIA*, CARVED PLAQUE COMMEMORATING LAUNCH

GREAT BRITAIN, 1906

Synonymous with tragedy and a defining moment of the First World War, Cunard's RMS *Lusitania* was born out of the early twentieth-century rivalry between Britain and Germany, who were challenging for dominance on the North Atlantic.

Built at John Brown and Co. on the Clyde, *Lusitania* was partly funded by a government loan to Cunard, on the basis that she, and her sister *Mauretania*, could be called into naval service in time of conflict. Launched on 7 June 1906, she was 31,550 GRT and 787 × 88ft. Her steam turbines produced 76,000hp. Her maiden voyage, Liverpool to New York, took place on 7 September and she

A carved plaque, possibly a shipyard apprentice piece, commemorating the launch of RMS Lusitania, 7 June 1906.

soon claimed the Blue Riband for Cunard on both the east–west and west–east runs. She and *Mauretania* were to trade this accolade between them, although *Mauretania* was to be consistently faster over their careers.

Her interior design retained a traditional style, with the usual three-class configuration, with 563 in first, 464 in second and 1,138 in third class, along with a crew of 802. In first class there were some stunning rooms, such as the lounge with its huge barrel-vaulted stained-glass ceiling and the two-deck dining room in the style of Louis Seize with a decorated plasterwork dome above. There were two first-class electric lifts. Second-class accommodation was as good as first class on earlier Cunarders, and third class was soon found to be a cut above most contemporary steamers. Overall, her interiors were more light and airy than her sister *Mauretania*.

So, *Lusitania* was fast, she was comfortable (although she did suffer from vibration problems) and she was popular. After the outbreak of war, *Lusitania* continued her North Atlantic service. She left New York for Liverpool on 1 May 1915. The Germans had declared the waters around Britain a war zone and posted newspaper advertisements to this effect. *Lusitania* sailed for home, her Cunard red funnels now painted black.

On the morning of Friday, 7 May, *Lusitania* entered the war zone. Hoping that her speed would protect her, Captain William Turner had the lifeboats swung out as a precaution anyway. At 12.10 p.m. she was struck on the starboard bow by a single torpedo from submarine *U-20*, which had been operating around Britain but was nearing the end of her patrol.

There was almost immediately a second larger explosion, which could have been her boilers, coal dust igniting in her bunkers, or ammunition that *Lusitania* was known to be carrying in her holds. She sank in just eighteen minutes off the Old Head of Kinsale,

Watercolour of RMS *Lusitania*.

Ireland, taking 1,198 men women and children with her, 128 of them American.

In the immediate aftermath, it was thought that perhaps British Admiralty (Winston Churchill was First Lord of the Admiralty) had allowed *Lusitania* to sail into harm's way in order that her loss, and that of American citizens aboard, might bring the US into the war. This was not the immediate case, but it started debate in the US and there is no question that it was a factor in the country declaring war on Germany on 6 April 1917. We will return to *Lusitania* in a later chapter.

Apprentice shipbuilders often worked on so-called apprentice pieces to showcase their growing skills within their chosen trade. The plaque may be an example of this, or could possibly have been carved as a gift for VIPs at the launch.

RMS *MAURETANIA*, PHOSPHOR BRONZE MODEL OF PROPELLER

GREAT BRITAIN, 1906

The boat-express is waiting your command!
You will find the *Mauretania* at the quay,
Till her captain turns the lever 'neath his hand,
And the monstrous nine-decked city goes to sea.

Rudyard Kipling

In the first years of the twentieth century, it became apparent that nations other than Britain were flexing their maritime muscles. Germany in particular gave cause for concern; by 1903 it possessed the four fastest merchant vessels afloat. In the US, J. Pierpont

RMS *Mauretania* propeller model.

Morgan's International Mercantile Marine combine also posed a commercial threat, as its acquisition of the White Star Line reinforced. The problem was not just the possible loss of trans-atlantic business to faster ships, but the government also had an eye to future conflict where fast armed merchant cruisers or troop ships under British control could be vital.

The result of this was the British government agreeing to a loan and subsidy to Cunard for the construction of *Mauretania* and *Lusitania*.

RMS *Mauretania* was launched at Swan Hunter on the Tyne on 20 September 1906. At 31,938 tons, she was 762 × 88ft and had four turbine engines plus a reversing turbine, linked to four screws. To produce steam, she had twenty-three double-ended and two single-ended boilers. Her designed speed was 25 knots.

The image shows a model of one of these phosphor-bronze propellers. On her initial trials, *Mauretania* was found to suffer from vibration at high speed; something that was not uncommon with a new liner. Without today's computer design technology, some problems did not manifest themselves until the ship was complete and put through trials. Alterations were made to the original propellers, and some strengthening and stiffening was carried out at the stern of the ship in order to address the problem.

This graceful ship had seven decks and could carry 560 first-, 475 second- and 1,300 third-class passengers. First-class accommodation featured a two-tiered dining room and veranda-café. Second and third class were comfortable for the time, and as with any liner of the time, *Mauretania* made her profits from the transport of immigrants to the New World.

The government stipulated a speed of 24.5 knots in moderate weather as a condition of the loan and subsidy; *Mauretania* proved to be faster. She and *Lusitania* traded the Blue Riband between 1907 and 1914, although the Maury was the faster overall:

Mauretania: The Ship and Her Record.

in September 1909 she crossed westbound in four days, ten hours and fifty-one minutes, averaging 26.06 knots. This record was to stand for twenty years!

War came and *Mauretania* was used for trooping, and made three voyages to Gallipoli. She was used as a hospital ship, bringing 6,298 wounded back from Mudros in September 1915, before returning to trooping. Her sister *Lusitania* did not survive the war, as discussed in other chapters.

In 1921–22 *Mauretania* returned to the Tyne for a complete refit and conversion to oil burning, making her easier to bunker and requiring less stokehold personnel. She continued to break records, and was painted white and sent cruising, but by 1934 she had been in service for twenty-eight years and was withdrawn from operation. On 4 July 1935 she arrived at Rosyth, and after being opened to the public one last time, scrapping began. By 1937 RMS *Mauretania* was gone.

Many of her fittings survive and one often comes across souvenir wooden pots, boxes and other pieces made from her decking, marked 'Mauretania – The Old Lady of the Atlantic'.

The model propeller was made in the late 1950s by metallurgy students at King's College, London, and presented to their professor, George McKray. It shows the amazing design and precision of the components that drove vast liners at such high speed.

5

OLYMPIC-CLASS LINERS, SOUVENIR NUMBER OF *THE SHIPBUILDER*

GREAT BRITAIN, 1911

The story of RMS *Titanic* is well known, told in a multitude of books films and documentaries. She was the second of three sister ships, known collectively as the Olympic class. *The Shipbuilder and Marine Engine Builder*, the respected industry periodical, published a special souvenir number in 1911 devoted to these huge, ground-breaking new liners.

As usual with the White Star Line, Harland and Wolff in Belfast was to build these liners, and *Olympic* was laid down in December 1908, and launched on 20 October 1910. *Titanic* was still under construc-tion on the adjacent slipway, and she would be launched on 31 May the following year. On launch, *Olympic* was the largest ship in the world, at 45,342 GRT and 882ft 9in × 92ft 6in. The design team was led by Thomas Andrews, managing director and chief designer at Harland and Wolff, who had joined in 1889 as an apprentice.

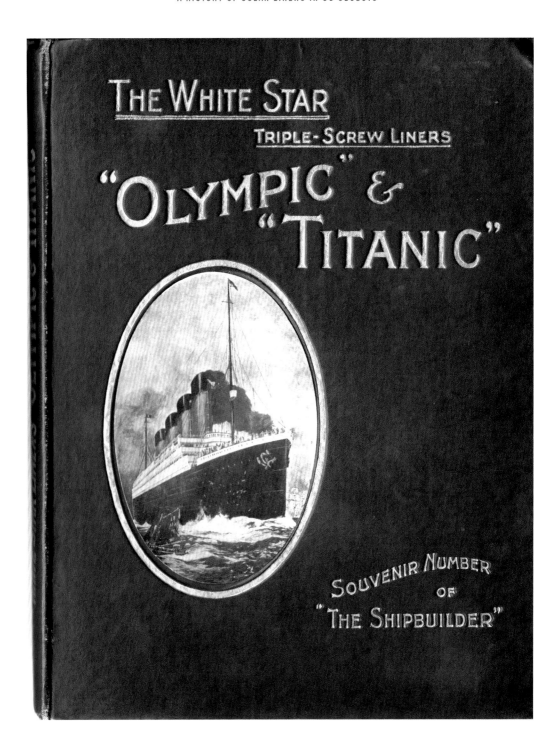

The Shipbuilder goes into immense detail concerning the construction of these ships. Three screws were driven by two huge reciprocating engines and a central turbine, powered by steam from twenty-nine coal-fired boilers, requiring thirty-five engineers and electricians and 176 leading stokers and stokers. The ships were divided into sixteen watertight compartments with electrically operated watertight doors that could be closed from the bridge and rendered the ship, according to *The Shipbuilder*, 'practically unsinkable'. Lifeboat regulations at the time did not stipulate that enough boats for all aboard needed to be carried. *Olympic* and *Titanic* were actually fitted with twenty boats, where they could have accommodated sixty-four. After the *Titanic* disaster, all shipping lines were forced to review their lifeboat arrangements.

The *Olympic* class were built for comfort and the quality of accommodation and facilities, and this applied to all three classes. From first class with deluxe suites with private balconies, a la carte dining, Turkish baths, indoor pool and lifts, to comfortable second class, which was the equivalent of first class on contemporary ships, these ships were unsurpassed. *The Shipbuilder* tells us that even third class had accommodation that was light, airy and of superior character. The dining room stretched for 100ft and seated 473. There was an oak-panelled smoking room and even staterooms in steerage generally only accommodated two to four people, a world away from the dormitory accommodation on other liners. Speed was a moderate 21 knots but these liners were not built to break speed records.

Only *Olympic* had a long career, serving in peace and war until being scrapped in 1935. *Titanic* was lost on her maiden crossing to New York after striking an iceberg and sinking on the night of 14/15 April 1912, with the loss of 1,514 passengers and crew.

Olympic and *Titanic* souvenir number of *The Shipbuilder and Marine Engine Builder*, 1911.

The third sister, *Britannic*, was launched on 26 February 1914 and immediately pressed into war service as a hospital ship. On the morning of 21 November 1916, in the Kea Channel in the Aegean, she struck a mine and sank in just under an hour. Some 1,035 were saved and thirty lost their lives. There were failures with two watertight doors that rendered *Britannic*'s watertight compartments unable to retain sufficient buoyancy to keep the vessel afloat.

Thomas Andrews, shown in the postcard, was on board *Titanic* heading the Guarantee Group of Harland and Wolff shipyard workers who took the maiden voyage to check on the ship and suggest further improvements. All of the group, including Andrews, were lost.

Fact: Violet Jessop was on board *Olympic* when she collided with HMS *Hawke* in September 1911. She was a stewardess on *Titanic* and survived, whereupon she joined *Britannic*'s crew and survived again. She died in 1971.

LATE Mr. THOMAS ANDREWS
(Managing Director of Messrs. Harland & Wolff), a victim of the "Titanic" Disaster, April, 1912.

Original postcard showing Thomas Andrews, designer of the Olympic-class liners.

SS *IMPERATOR*, MAIDEN VOYAGE MEDAL AND BROCHURE

GERMANY, 1912

Another example of the way competition between nations led to bigger and more luxurious liners was the massive *Imperator*. She was launched on 23 May 1912 at AG Vulcan Stettin after being christened by Kaiser Wilhelm II himself. A medal was struck to commemorate the launch of the new ship, together with a brochure portraying the power and luxury of the new liner.

Imperator was operated by the Hamburg Amerika Line. She was the first of a class of three liners, all in excess of 50,000 tons, and over 900ft in length. The other two were to be named *Vaterland* and *Bismarck*, with the three liners conceived by Hapag's visionary managing director, Albert Ballin.

These ships surpassed the White Star Line *Olympic* class in all respects, although like those ships, none of the Imperator class ever

Medal commemorating *Imperator*, 1913, by C. Kuhl.

took the Blue Riband. With a service speed of around 22.5 knots, however, they were by no means slow. *Imperator* was a four-screw, coal-fired turbine liner and could produce 62,000hp, more than *Olympic* or the new *Aquitania*.

Not only in size, but also in luxury, these ships surpassed everything with which they had to compete. *Imperator* could carry 4,248 passengers divided into four classes. Her crew totalled 1,180. First-class accommodation on *Imperator* took up most of her length and incorporated a 23m-long ballroom, Ritz-Carlton restaurant and a massive 8m-high, two-level domed dining room. There was a winter garden and a lavish indoor pool measuring 65 × 41ft in Pompeian style, whilst electric lifts took passengers between decks. Even in fourth or steerage class, which could house 1,772 passengers, there were simple rooms with multiple bunks rather than the dormitories that were standard on other ships.

After the loss of *Titanic* in April, all shipping companies had to reappraise lifesaving provision, and *Imperator* carried fifty-six lifeboats, fourteen collapsible boats and six launches.

One of *Imperator*'s most striking external features was the eagle. Perched on her bow and gripping a globe in its talons, this massive bronze figurehead was designed by Professor Bruno Kruse of Berlin. A prominent symbol of German imperialism, this feature also ensured that *Imperator* was slightly longer than Cunard's *Aquitania*, then under construction. The eagle had its wings clipped during a 1914 crossing when it was badly damaged in a storm. The rest of the unlucky and by now sorry-looking bird was subsequently removed.

The ship's maiden voyage from Cuxhaven to New York via Southampton took place on 10 June 1913, and some stability issues emerged that had to be addressed by her builders.

A long career serving her owners was not to be. War broke out in August 1914 and *Imperator* was laid up in Hamburg for the duration. After the Armistice, she was taken by the Allies and used

Early brochure, SS *Imperator.*

The eagle mounted on the bow.

to transport American service personnel back to the US, moving around 25,000 personnel across the Atlantic. Under the Treaty of Versailles, a huge portion of the remaining German merchant fleet was to be given to the victorious powers, and *Imperator* was transferred to Great Britain in September 1919, partly as reparation for the loss of RMS *Lusitania* in 1915.

A new life awaited *Imperator*. Taken over by Cunard, she was to be returned to service for her new owners as quickly as possible, but was found to be in far worse condition than anticipated. Renamed *Berengaria*, she would become the flagship of the Cunard Line. We will resume her story in another chapter.

RMS *AQUITANIA*, BRASS BELL

GREAT BRITAIN, 1914

The small bell opposite is made from metal from *Aquitania*, a long-lived and much loved Cunarder. Known as 'The Ship Beautiful', this majestic four-funnelled liner was considerably larger than the earlier *Lusitania* and *Mauretania*. At 45,647 GRT, she was 901 × 97ft, quadruple-screw, turbine-driven and launched at John Brown & Co., Clydebank, on 21 April 1913.

Aquitania was designed as a response to White Star's Olympic class. Big, luxurious (for first class), with a maximum speed of 23 knots, she could carry 3,200 passengers in three classes with a crew of 972.

The interiors of the ship were ornate to say the least. Designed by Mewes and Davis, who also worked on German liners, the traditional style was very much in evidence. The stunning columned Palladian

Bell made to commemorate *Aquitania*'s thirty-five years of service.

lounge actually had a huge ceiling painting removed from a Dutch country house. There was a restaurant in the style of Louis XVI, and other styles included Jacobean, while there were also echoes of Christopher Wren. Cunard actually published a 200-page book in 1914, written by A.M. Broadley, that solely showcasing the ship's interiors, with many illustrations and somewhat flowery descriptions of each interior space. No other liner appears to have had so much descriptive praise lavished on it in one volume.

From the book, Broadley quotes the following statistics in relation to the on-board service:

Cups and saucers – 20,000
Plates and covers – 22,000
Glasses and tumblers – 12,000
Knives, forks and carvers – 15,000
Spoons – 15,000
Jugs, decanters and carafes – 5,000
Cruets, bottles, mustard pots, egg hoops and salts – 4,250
Dishes (meat, vegetables, boats, moulds, etc) – 10,000
Toast racks and escalloped shells – 1,100

Aquitania's maiden voyage from Liverpool started on 30 May 1914 and she arrived at New York on 5 June. Her captain was William Turner, later to be in command of the *Lusitania* on her final voyage. After only three return crossings, the outbreak of war on 4 August curtailed the new liner's civilian career and she was converted in only four days to an auxiliary cruiser. After a collision with a Leyland Line ship on 25 August, she was withdrawn from this unsuitable use, laid up then and repurposed as a troop ship, serving in the Dardanelles campaign. She was painted in dazzle colours to camouflage her against submarine attack, and later repainted in hospital ship colours as she carried 25,000 wounded back home from the Mediterranean. She was back to trooping on the entry of the US into the war.

After the war she was refitted, converted to oil burning and returned to service alongside *Mauretania* and *Berengaria* (ex-German SS *Imperator*). Cunard and White Star merged in December 1934, and *Aquitania* sailed under the new joint flag.

By the mid 1930s *Aquitania* was showing her age, and two new Cunarders, *Queen Mary* (1934) and *Queen Elizabeth* (1938), were about to appear. The war gave her a reprieve and she spent the next eight years trooping everywhere from Australia to Singapore, and to and from the US, also taking war brides to Canada in 1948. This was to be the end. Tired, uneconomical to maintain and meet new regulations, she was scrapped in Faslane, Scotland, after thirty-five years of service in peace and war.

The small bell in the image, made from metal and wood recovered from the ship by Metal Industries Ltd of Faslane, Scotland, is inscribed 'May 1914–Feb 1950', in commemoration of *Aquitania*'s many years of service. Ship breakers would often produce items such as this as souvenirs of famous ships that they had dismantled.

8

RMS *BERENGARIA*, SALOON CHAIR

GREAT BRITAIN, 1921

After the First World War, the mighty *Imperator*, which had lain at Hamburg for the duration, was pressed into service by the US as a troop transport. She transported 28,000 personnel before, in August 1919, she was transferred to British ownership, to be run by Cunard.

Named RMS *Imperator*, her funnels now painted in Cunard red and black, she sailed from the US for Southampton on 21 December, but on arrival it was found that she was in need of a much larger amount of work and refurbishment than originally thought. It was March 1920 before she was refitted and put under the command of Arthur Rostron of *Carpathia/Titanic* fame. She ran as *Imperator* until

Berengaria chair.

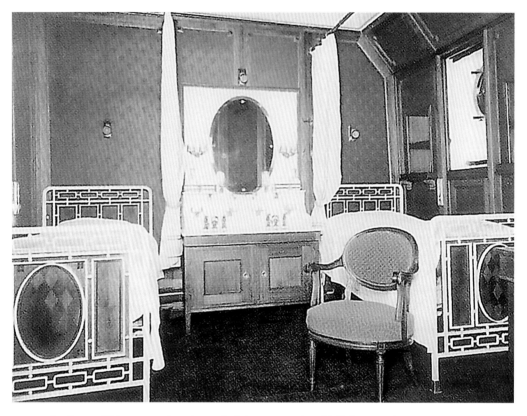

A suite on SS *Imperator* showing a chair later reused on RMS *Berengaria*.

February 1921, when she became *Berengaria*. Cunard liners always had names with the suffix 'ia', just as White Star Liners names ended with 'ic'. *Berengaria* was the wife of Richard the Lionheart.

Berengaria became a popular liner on the North Atlantic and she had a huge capacity, being able to carry 4,000 passengers and crew. During the Great Depression, as with other liners, she had to adapt to changing times. In 1931, she ran short four-day 'prohibition avoidance' cruises from New York, and these fitted in between transatlantic turnarounds. Things did not improve however, and in September 1932 she sailed eastbound from New York with only 134 passengers aboard. By 1934, the situation started to look better, and in that year *Berengaria* became part of the new merger between Cunard and White Star. Up to that point, she had been the Cunard Line flagship.

Throughout her career, *Berengaria* had suffered from wiring problems, which led to numerous small fires. In a three-week period in February/March 1938 two fires broke out on board, causing much more extensive damage than previous blazes, and this culminated in the US authorities refusing to grant her a certificate of seaworthiness. On 21 March 1938, it was announced that *Berengaria* was to be withdrawn from service. The newer *Queen Mary* was now operating, and *Queen Elizabeth* was nearing completion.

She was sold for £500,000 and made her final voyage from Southampton on 6 December, for Jarrow. The war interrupted her demolition, and she did not finally fully disappear until 1946.

The image shows a dining or saloon chair from *Berengaria*. This style of chair can be seen in publicity brochures for the original *Imperator* and again in photographs of the interiors of *Berengaria*. There are photographs of the chairs after being bought for the new Middleton Tower Holiday Camp near Morecambe, northern England, after the ship was scrapped. Part of the complex was a huge theatre and leisure building, designed to look like an ocean liner and named 'SS Berengaria'. The park closed in 1994 and the *Berengaria* building was demolished.

Furniture and fittings for ocean liners were finely crafted and built to last through the rigours of a long ocean-going career. It is perhaps no surprise that pieces such as this chair have survived down the years. From the height of Imperial Germany via triumphant Cunard days on the North Atlantic, to a holiday camp in northern England. What a fascinating history and legacy the liners leave behind.

9

SS *ÎLE DE FRANCE*, CUTAWAY RENDERING

FRANCE, 1926

Appearances can be deceptive! Outwardly a traditional three-funnelled interwar liner, the French Line's *Île De France* was quite revolutionary. She is seen as the beginning of the 'moderne' style of liner design, which would be universally adopted in the 1930s for ships, architecture and couture, eventually becoming what we now call art deco.

The roots of this style can be traced back to the early twentieth century when a group of radical French designers lobbied the government to host a world's fair to showcase a new wave of artists, sculptors, architects and designers. The First World War meant that this Great Exposition could not be held until 1925. Paris was the venue for this paean to modernism, which was named Exposition Internationale des arts Décoratifs et Industriels Modernes. A number of pavilions showcased design from twenty countries.

The direct result for ocean liner design was that the French Line, formally called Compagnie Générale Transatlantique or CGT, embraced the style and spirit of the Exposition and commissioned artists and designers such as Pierre Patout and Raymond Subes to work on the new liner. There was a three-storey marble-clad hall with a double staircase allowing for a grand entrance. There were marble columns, Aubusson tapestries, decorative ironwork and marquetry panelling. The moderne French theme was carried through every design feature, from the chairs in the salon to the silverware in the dining rooms. Hollywood loved the Île; she was exciting, a break from the old ideas of recreating the feel of a country house at sea, she had her own 'liner style', and soon had a loyal following.

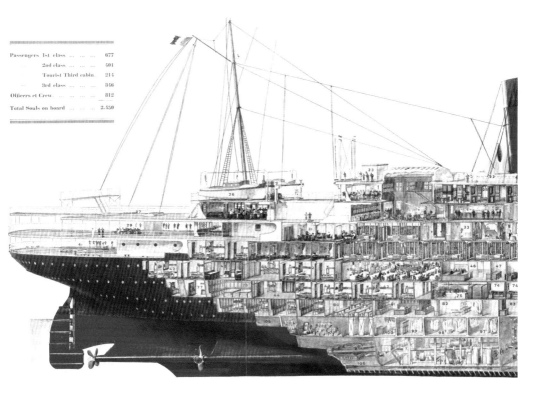

Passengers 1st class 677
2nd class 404
Tourist Third cabin. 214
3rd class 346
Officers et Crew 812
Total Souls on board 2,450

Launched in 1926, she was 792 × 91.9ft and 43,153 GRT. Turbine-driven, she could accommodate 537 first, 603 second, and 646 third class with 800 crew. After service in the Second World War she was extensively remodelled and reconfigured with two funnels. Her first post-war voyage, Le Havre to New York, was on 21 July 1949. She soon regained her reputation for service and style, and had apparently lost none of her pre-war individuality. Her cuisine was legendary – it was said that more seagulls followed the *Ile* for scraps than any other liner!

Île De France settled into a new phase of transatlantic service. In 1953 she rescued the crew of a sinking cargo ship, *Greenville*. On 26 July 1956, she was in attendance to help the stricken *Andrea Doria* as she sank off Nantucket. The *Île* rescued 753 people.

COMPAGNIE GÉNÉRALE TRANSATLANTIQUE

French Line

SECTIONAL VIEW OF THE LINER " ILE DE FRANCE

Finally, in 1958 she was sold to scrappers in Osaka, Japan. She had one final role to play, as SS *Claridon*, a sinking liner in the 1960 film *The Last Voyage*. *Île De France* was partially sunk in shallow water off Osaka, explosions were rigged and a funnel made to collapse. Many scenes were shot on board. The French Line was appalled by the treatment of their former flagship, but this was her final indignity, and a few months later she was no more.

Many shipping companies, especially the French Line, commissioned artists to create cutaway renderings of their ships, strikingly bringing to life the beehive of activity, public rooms, cabins and engineering spaces. These were distributed to travel agents and on board.

Original French Line cutaway of *Île De France*.

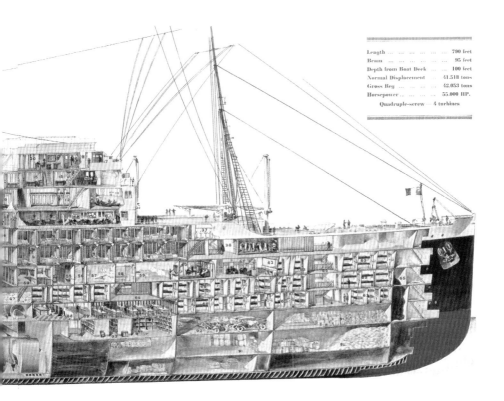

Length ... ... 790 feet
Beam ... ... 95 feet
Depth from Boat Deck ... ... 100 feet
Normal Displacement ... 41,518 tons
Gross Reg ... ... 42,053 tons
Horsepower .. .. 55,000 HP.
Quadruple-screw — 4 turbines

10

BREMEN AND EUROPA, SOUVENIR CIGAR BOX

GERMANY, 1928

Germany launched these two super liners within a day of each other in August 1928. *Europa* was built by the Blohm and Voss yard, Hamburg, at just shy of 50,000 tons, 941 × 102ft, while *Bremen*, slightly larger at 51,656 tons, was launched from AG Weser, Bremen.

These two oil-fired turbine steamers were operated by North German Lloyd made clear Germany's resurgence post-First World War and they were built for speed! Furthermore, they embraced the new post-war design sensibilities and moved away from the dour 'Teutonic' style towards a more streamlined, modernist and avant-garde feel. Another feature was that each ship carried a seaplane launched from a catapult mounted between the funnels. One day out from either New York or Cherbourg, the plane would be despatched, bringing the mail ashore well before the ship docked.

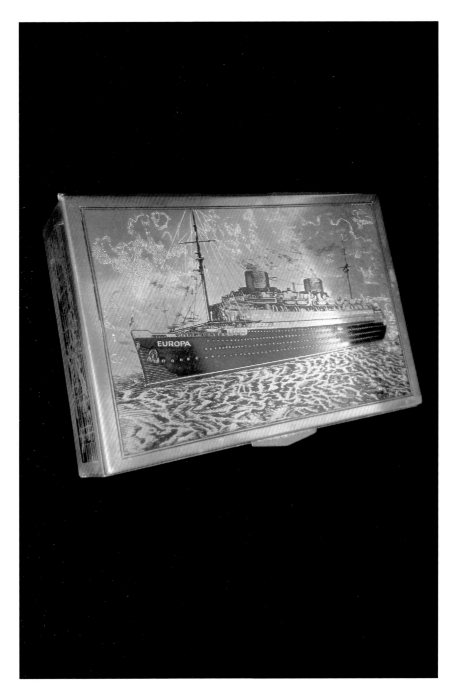

Europa souvenir cigarette or cigar box, etched brass.

Model of SS *Bremen* by Classic Ship Collection.

Bremen began her maiden voyage from Bremerhaven to New York on 16 July 1929, taking the Blue Riband both west and east-bound with an average speed of 27.83 and 27.91 knots respectively. *Europa* suffered a mysterious and extensive fire before being completed and so her maiden voyage was delayed until March 1930. She captured the westbound Blue Riband from her sister with an average speed of 27.91 knots.

Although luxurious, fast and technically impressive, neither ship carried as many passengers as forecast. Not only was the Great Depression having an effect on the transatlantic trade generally, but anti-German feeling grew as the Nazis' grip on power in Germany increased, and these ships both flew the Swastika.

Two days before Germany invaded Poland, *Bremen* left New York without passengers, and during the voyage was painted camouflage grey. She maintained radio silence and made her way stealthily to Bremerhaven, taking a circuitous route via Murmansk and the Norwegian coast. Here she joined *Europa* and, with war now officially declared, there were plans to turn both ships into troop transports, as the invasion of Britain was being planned, dependent only on Herman Goering's Luftwaffe gaining control of the skies.

Neither ship was to sail for Germany again. *Bremen* was set alight by a disgruntled crewman on 16 March 1941. She was gutted and filled with water from firefighters' efforts to extinguish the blaze. Beyond salvage, *Bremen* was cut up where she lay. *Europa* spent the war neglected and rusting in Bremerhaven, but as we will see in another chapter, she would have a rebirth and a whole new life beyond the war.

The image shows a brass cigarette or cigar box, with a detailed etching of *Europa* and a wooden lining. This would have been bought in the ship's on-board boutique, and is a good example of the quality, and no doubt considerable cost, of some of these souvenir items. Shipping companies have always made it possible to buy all manner of branded merchandise on board. Bud vases and powder compacts featuring a company crest or image of the ship were particularly popular. On a modern liner, one can buy everything from models of the ships to tins of mints, and even company-branded gin!

MV BRITANNIC, LIFEBOAT PLAQUE

GREAT BRITAIN, 1929

The object shown is an original name plaque that was fitted to a lifeboat from MV *Britannic*. The prefix MV denotes a motor vessel, which in the case of *Britannic* meant diesel engines driving twin screws. She was the first motor ship to be ordered by White Star.

Ordered in 1928, *Britannic* and her sister ship *Georgic* were both built at Harland and Wolff, Belfast, and were the last two liners to be built for the White Star Line. Designed as a cabin- and tourist-class liner, *Britannic* was intended for the Liverpool to New York run in the summer and would go cruising in winter. She was completed as quickly as possible to replace the older liner *Celtic* (1901), which had recently run aground and been lost at Roches Point, Ireland.

Britannic was an intermediate-size liner, at 26,943 GRT and 712 × 82.3ft. Not designed for speed, she cruised at around

MV *Britannic* lifeboat plaque.

17.5 knots, but was economical and carried more than 1,500 passengers and 500 crew. The three classes were Cabin, Tourist and third. In fact, there was little difference between the first two classes. Her interiors were very much of a traditional period style, whereas the slightly newer *Georgic* had a more modern art deco style. Britannic could also carry cargo and was also able to transport motor vehicles.

Britannic's Maiden Liverpool–New York voyage took place on 28 June 1930 and she soon became a success, although the bigger picture for the White Star Line was not good, and by 1934, after suffering considerable losses, White Star merged with Cunard. *Britannic* and *Georgic* were the only two White Star ships to join the new line, Cunard/White Star, and by 1949 the White Star name would vanish completely. However, *Britannic* and *Georgic* were allowed to display the White Star burgee alongside the Cunard house flag until the end of their careers.

During the war, *Britannic* served, as did many liners, as a troopship. She steamed to Bombay, Africa, Suez, and took American troops to the landings in Sicily. She also brought US troops to

Cunard White Star   *Britannic*

Britain for the D-Day landings. She came through undamaged, whereas *Georgic* was badly damaged by aircraft in Suez in July 1941.

After the war came a year-long refit before she resumed her peacetime role. Her interiors were rebuilt in a more modern style. The 'cabin'-type liners became popular and profitable. The express liners such as *Queen Mary* and *Elizabeth* were expensive to run and were operating at a loss. *Britannic* was to spend the next twelve years crossing the Atlantic in summer and cruising the Mediterranean in winter.

Georgic was scrapped in February 1956. *Britannic* carried on until December 1960, when still displaying the White Star flag, the last liner ever to do so, she sailed to Inverkeithing to be broken up. The White Star Line, which had operated since Thomas Ismay acquired the name in 1868, the line that had operated *Oceanic*, *Olympic* and *Titanic*, finally disappeared from the seas.

SS L'ATLANTIQUE,
FIRST-CLASS TABLE NUMBER

FRANCE, 1930

If there was ever a liner whose exterior so belied what lay within, it was *L'Atlantique*.

Ordered by Compagnie de Navigation Sud Atlantique for the lucrative run from France to South America, she was designed to be able to navigate both the Gironde River in France (Bordeaux) and the River Plate in South America (Buenos Aires). This meant that she was wide in the beam compared to her length, and had a high superstructure, giving her a less than streamlined appearance. Her three oddly spaced funnels gave her a somewhat ungainly look. She was the biggest liner on the Europe–South America run, being 42,512 GRT and 744 × 92ft. Her capacity was 414 first class, 158 second class and 584 third class, with a crew of 663. She was a quadruple-screw, turbine-driven vessel with a maximum speed of around 24 knots.

Art-deco style! This first-class silver table number from SS *L'Atlantique* perfectly shows the moderne style that the ship encapsulated.

Inside, *L'Atlantique* was a design marvel. Built with money guaranteed by state bonds, designers Pierre Patout, who was to work on the *Normandie*, and Messrs Rageunet et Maillard created interiors that would resonate within ocean liner design for years to come. What was known in the 1930s as streamline moderne is now famously known as art deco.

One huge constraint in ocean liner design is the need for funnel uptakes. On most ships up to then, these would run up through the middle of the ship, necessitating public rooms becoming disjointed as they had to work around the division of these massive central voids. On *L'Atlantique*, these uptakes were taken up each side of the hull internally, allowing for huge, interconnecting public spaces. These rooms on *L'Atlantique* included a 35m, two-storey dining room, and an ornate grand salon with adjoining oval salon with glass dome and rosewood pillars. We will return to the use of wood on ocean liners in other chapters.

One of the most revolutionary features of the ship was the 'Rue de la Paix'. This street of shops ran for 137m through E-deck with two balcony levels above overlooking the street. At 5m wide and 9m high, there were more than forty boutiques selling clothing, perfumes, shoes and many other luxuries, as well as more practical merchandise. There was extensive use of marble and walnut panel-ling, and the whole space was beautifully lit and had a contrasting red, black and white carpet.

When you board a modern cruise ship and admire the impres-sive multi-deck atrium, or stroll through a vast shopping and dining space with cafés and outlets, it all began with *L'Atlantique*.

Her career was not a long one. Launched in April 1930, she ran only ten voyages before catching fire 23 miles off Guernsey in January 1933. All but eighteen of the reduced passage crew of 223 were rescued and the ship drifted in the Channel, derelict. She was sighted from the English south coast. Eventually towed to

Obverse, Amphitrite, Goddess of the Sea. Reverse, *L'Atlantique* steaming at sea.

Cherbourg, this gorgeous liner was scrapped in Greenock, Scotland, in 1936. There were reports of previous fires and warnings of sabotage, together with suspicions about sub-standard wiring and comments about use of wood and other highly combustible materials in her construction. Whatever the cause of the fire, *L'Atlantique* was stunningly appointed and tragically short-lived.

Rue de la paiz

RMS *STRATHNAVER*, LAUNCH MENU

GREAT BRITAIN, 1931

The launch of any liner is an occasion for celebration. The long period of design and construction of the hull is complete and it is time for the ship to enter her natural environment. TSS *Strathnaver* was no exception and a dinner was held at the ship builders post launch; the launch itself was done by Lady Janet Bailey, who was the daughter of P&O chairman Lord Inchcape.

The first of five 'White Sisters', *Strathnaver* was part of P&O's evolution of the service from Tilbury to Australia via the Suez Canal.

Launched on 5 February 1931 at Vickers-Armstrongs Ltd, Barrow, she was the first P&O liner to be painted white with three distinctive buff funnels, although only the middle funnel served any purpose. A liner's speed and safety was judged by the public on the amount of funnels she carried, hence many liners of the early to mid-twentieth century carried a dummy (or two).

Strathnaver was 638 × 80ft and 22,283 GRT. Her twin screws were driven by a turbo-electric power plant giving her around 22 knots. Designed as a two-class ship, she could carry 498 in first class and 670 in tourist class.

Despite the savage downturn in world trade at the time, it was hoped that *Strathnaver* and her sisters would serve the company well. She left on her maiden voyage, fully booked, on 1 October 1931, sailing from Tilbury to Marseilles, and then transiting the Suez Canal on 14/15 October, managing to run aground in the process. She then called at Aden, Bombay (Mumbai), Colombo, Fremantle and Adelaide. She was the biggest liner to dock at Sydney when she arrived on 12 November. Her final call was Brisbane, and then back to Tilbury, arriving in January, just as her new sister, *Strathaird*, entered service.

Strathnaver was fairly traditional in her interior design. Principal public rooms were panelled in cedar and oak with Queen Anne oak furniture. There was something of a Scottish feel to the reading and writing room with its panel depicting Bonnie Prince Charlie. Tourist class also had attractive wood-panelled dining and reception rooms, and there was a wash basin with hot and cold running water in each cabin. *Strathnaver* was one of the first ships to offer a standard of tourist-class accommodation that was only slightly less well appointed than first.

Strathnaver was well-suited to cruising, with lots of sports deck space and a swimming pool. She ran Mediterranean and Baltic cruises as well as visiting the Pacific, including New Zealand and Fiji.

War took her on trooping duties, transporting Australian and New Zealand troops to the Middle East. In November 1942 she took part in Operation Torch, landing troops at Algiers, and was at the Anzio landings in 1944. She repatriated troops post-war and returned to

LAUNCH OF

T.S.S. "STRATHNAVER"

BY

LADY JANET BAILEY,

AT THE

NAVAL CONSTRUCTION WORKS,

BARROW-IN-FURNESS.

5th February, 1931.

RMS *Strathnaver* launch menu.

MENU.

Turtle Soup.

———

Boiled Salmon.　Fillets of Sole.

———

Roast Lamb.　Mint Sauce.
Roast Chicken.　York Ham.

———

Asparagus.

———

Charlotte Russe,
Meringues.
Plum Pudding.　Camperdown Sauce.

———

Scotch Woodcock.

———

Dessert.

———

Coffee.

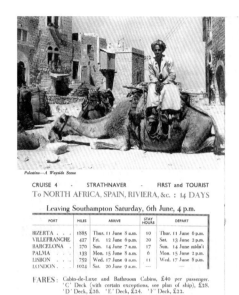

Palestine—A Wayside Scene

CRUISE 5 - STRATHAIRD - FIRST AND TOURIST
TO CORFU, ATHENS, MALTA, &c. : 14 DAYS

Leaving London Friday, 12th June, 4.30 p.m.

PORT	MILES	ARRIVE	STAY HOURS	DEPART
CORFU . . .	2582	Thur. 18 June 8 a.m.	5	Thur. 18 June 1 p.m.
ATHENS . . .	369	Fri. 19 June 8 a.m.	12	Fri. 19 June 8 p.m.
MALTA . . .	517	Sun. 21 June 7 a.m.	6	Sun. 21 June 1 p.m.
SOUTHAMPTON	2120	Fri. 26 June 2 p.m.	—	

FARES : Cabin-de-Luxe and Bathroom Cabins, £40 per passenger.
'C' Deck (with certain exceptions, see plan of ship), £28.
'D' Deck, £26. 'E' Deck, £24. 'F' Deck, £22.
Tourist Class : £13 and £16.

CRUISE 4 - STRATHNAVER - FIRST and TOURIST
To NORTH AFRICA, SPAIN, RIVIERA, &c. : 14 DAYS

Leaving Southampton Saturday, 6th June, 4 p.m.

PORT	MILES	ARRIVE	STAY HOURS	DEPART
BIZERTA . . .	1885	Thur. 11 June 8 a.m.	10	Thur. 11 June 6 p.m.
VILLEFRANCHE	427	Fri. 12 June 6 p.m.	20	Sat. 13 June 2 p.m.
BARCELONA .	270	Sun. 14 June 7 a.m.	17	Sun. 14 June midn't
PALMA . . .	133	Mon. 15 June 8 a.m.	6	Mon. 15 June 2 p.m.
LISBON . . .	752	Wed. 17 June 0 a.m.	11	Wed. 17 June 8 p.m.
LONDON . . .	1024	Sat. 20 June 9 a.m.	—	

FARES : Cabin-de-Luxe and Bathroom Cabins, £40 per passenger.
'C' Deck (with certain exceptions, see plan of ship), £28.
'D' Deck, £26. 'E' Deck, £24. 'F' Deck, £22.
Tourist Class : £13 and £16.

CRUISE 7 - STRATHAIRD - FIRST AND TOURIST
TO N. AFRICA, SPAIN and PORTUGAL : 13 DAYS

Leaving Southampton Saturday, 27th June, 4 p.m.

PORT	MILES	ARRIVE	STAY HOURS	DEPART
BIZERTA . . .	1885	Thur. 2 July 8 a.m.	11	Thur. 2 July 7 p.m.
MALTA . . .	242	Fri. 3 July 9 a.m.	9	Fri. 3 July 6 p.m.
BARCELONA .	666	Sun. 5 July 7 a.m.	13	Sun. 5 July 8 p.m.
LISBON . . .	817	Tues. 7 July 7 p.m.	18	Wed. 8 July 1 p.m.
SOUTHAMPTON	866	Fri. 10 July 2 p.m.	—	

FARES : Cabin-de-Luxe and Bathroom Cabins, £40 per passenger.
'C' Deck (with certain exceptions, see plan of ship), £28.
'D' Deck, £26. 'E' Deck, £24. 'F' Deck, £22.
Tourist Class : £12 and £15.

Belfast for refitting, and the removal of the two dummy funnels. In 1954 she was converted to a one-class ship, with a capacity for 1,252 tourist passengers.

Strathnaver was sold in February 1962, and arrived in Hong Kong for scrapping in April. By then, another P&O White Ship, *Canberra*, had entered service.

Strathnaver, 1931–62 (scrapped)

Strathaird, 1932–61 (scrapped)

Strathmore, 1935–63 (scrapped)

Stratheden, 1937–64 (scrapped)

Strathallan, 1938–42 (torpedoed 21 December 1942)

P&O cruise brochure 1930s.

SS *REX*, ENTERTAINMENT PROGRAMME

ITALY, 1932

SS *Rex*, like many liners of the interwar period, was born into the period of the Great Depression. Starting with the Wall Street Crash of October 1929, the depression continued on into the 1930s. Many nations stopped building new ocean liners, and construction of RMS *Queen Mary* was halted from the end of 1931 to May 1934.

In spite of economic turmoil, *Rex* was launched on 1 August 1931. She was turbine driven and, at 51,062 GRT and 880 × 97ft, the largest ship to have been built in Italy. She was designed to run from Genoa to New York. This track was an additional two days compared to a crossing from Southampton to New York, but was known as the Sunny Southern Route. This meant that she and her sister, *Conti di Savoia*, were designed with large lido decks, swimming pools, promenades and terraces to encourage passengers to enjoy the warmer, calmer

SS *Rex* entertainment programme.

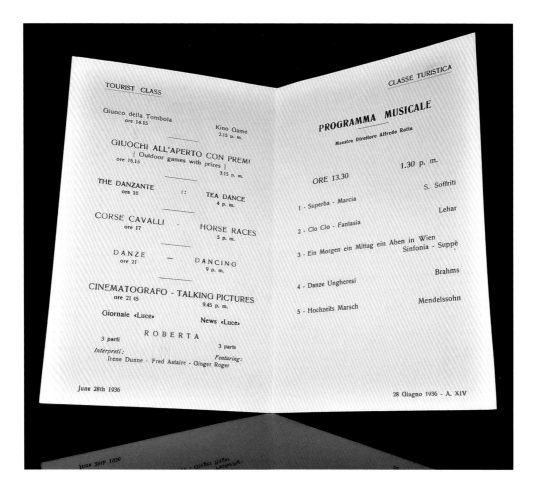

conditions to be expected on the crossing. Some of her suites had private verandas. The two ships were known as 'The Riviera Afloat'.

Rex was fairly conservative in her interior design, being more 'classic liner' than 'moderne'. She sailed on her maiden voyage on 27 September 1932 but engine problems held her up at Gibraltar for three days. Better was to come, however. After leaving Genoa on 10 August 1933, she took the Hales trophy, snatching the Blue Riband from *Bremen* with a crossing of four days, thirteen hours and fifty-eight minutes, averaging 28.92 knots. She was to keep the trophy until losing it to the French Line's *Normandie* two years later.

SS *Rex* stationery.

Not surprisingly, *Rex*, with her 10,000sq.m. of lido deck space, was ideally suited to cruising. She carried out a Christmas cruise to the West Indies in December 1932, and a Mediterranean cruise in February 1934. In February 1938 she cruised to Rio during the famous carnival.

War was to put an end to *Rex*, as with so many interwar liners. Her final transatlantic crossing saw her back in Genoa on 20 May 1940. She spent some time in Pula as an accommodation ship for shipyard workers before being laid up in Trieste until September 1944. After the Italian armistice she was taken by the Germans, stripped and towed off the coast, anchored and abandoned. On 8 September the ship was attacked by the RAF, who fired incendiary rockets into the ship until she burned and rolled onto her port side in the shallows. She was broken up over the next ten years.

Her sister *Conti di Savoia* suffered a similar fate, being attacked by Allied aircraft in September 1943. She was eventually raised but it was not economical to return her to service and she was scrapped in 1950.

This entertainment program and writing paper from *Rex* tell of happy days on the 'Sunny Southern Route' across the Atlantic. Even on a warmer route, not all on board activities revolved around Lido decks and pools: tourist class could also enjoy dances, talking pictures and classical music.

NORMANDIE, LALIQUE WATER GOBLET

FRANCE, 1932

In this book there are frequent references to this amazing French liner. She is considered by many to be the epitome of the inter-war ocean liner and indeed stands to this day as the most admired vessel of all time for her design and style.

In the late 1920s many nations were joining the race to build their own ships of state, and *Rex, Queen Mary*, *Bremen* and *Europa* were all born of this period. The French Line looked to an evolution of *Île De France* and conceived, at that time, the largest ship in the world, *Normandie*.

Launched on 29 October 1932 at Chantiers de Penhoet, St Nazaire, by Madame Lebrun, France's First Lady, *Normandie* was 1,030 × 117.8ft and 79,280 GRT. Quadruple screws were linked to a massive 165,000shp turbo-electric power plant. This and her

Lalique water goblet from a deluxe suite on SS *Normandie*.

revolutionary hull design, conceived by Russian designer Vladimir Yourkevitch, allowed her to average around 30 knots. Externally, her decks were uncluttered by ventilators or unnecessary deck fittings. She was very much the embodiment of streamline moderne, with her three huge, raked funnels, the rear of which was a dummy housing dog kennels.

On her maiden voyage on 29 May 1935, *Normandie* broke the record and claimed the Blue Riband from *Rex*, on both west and eastbound crossings. Over the next few years, *Normandie* was to trade the record with Cunard's *Queen Mary*.

In spite of the world economic situation, the French government pumped money into the project, and *Normandie* was completed where *Queen Mary*'s build was stalled. *Normandie*, at $60 million, cost over twice as much as the Cunarder. It might seem amazing now, but *Normandie* represented the best of French culture and design, and the money lavished on her was astounding for the time. Companies such as Lalique (glassware), Christofle (silverware) and Aubusson (carpeting and tapestries) were involved, along with designers such as Raymond Subes and Jean Dupas, who created stunning spaces such as the first-class dining room, glass clad, with Lalique glass lighting towers and longer than the Hall of Mirrors at Versailles. There was a grand lounge, winter garden, theatre, café-grill and indoor pool. Funnel uptakes running up the sides of the ship allowed an uninterrupted vista of 700ft, down the grand staircase, through lounges and salons, the length of the ship. There were staterooms, suites and deluxe suites, attracting celebrities and royalty. Tourist class had its own stunning dining room and even third class was well appointed, but there was no doubt that *Normandie*'s accommodation was geared to the premier-class experience and nothing was spared in that regard.

The times she was born into never allowed *Normandie* to fulfil her financial potential. She took two cruises to Rio, also calling at

Small bronze plaque, which is a replica of huge mural in the main dining room by Raymond Delamarre.

Original painting of SS *Normandie* arriving at New York by Harley Crossley.

Trinidad, Barbados and Martinique. On the 1939 cruise, famous artiste Carmen Miranda, then unknown, was invited to perform on board, having been spotted with her band at the Cassino da Urca in Rio. This discovery was the start of her stellar career.

The outbreak of war found *Normandie* in New York, and she was mothballed, with a skeleton crew to await the future. In December 1941, the US took her over, cleared her of her finery and began her conversion to a troop ship. Able to carry 14,000 troops, she was renamed *Lafayette*. On 9 February, during removal of the 'Fountains of Light' fixtures in the grand salon, welders ignited a pile of kapok life preservers and fire took hold. Over the next few hours, firefighters pumped water into the ship, and the next day she heeled over onto her side, resting in the mud alongside the pier.

After extensive removal of her superstructure, she was righted in August 1943, but tragically she was beyond repair, and in October 1943 the great *Normandie* was towed to Port Newark for scrapping.

She lives on in memory and, luckily, a huge amount of her original fixtures and fittings survive, to be found in museums worldwide and in the hands of private collectors. The glass shown is by Lalique, specially designed for her deluxe suites. The bronze is a small replica of a huge mural by Raymond Delamarre, which was placed at the entrance to the first-class dining room.

RMS *QUEEN MARY*, CHAD VALLEY MODEL

GREAT BRITAIN, 1934

The iconic ocean liner RMS *Queen Mary* had a difficult birth. Laid down on the Clyde at John Brown & Co. in December 1930, her construction halted a year later as the future of such a giant ship was thrown in to doubt owing to the worldwide economic downturn. After two years, the British government allowed Cunard to finance the completion of the ship by way of a loan, and Hull 534, as she was known, became RMS *Queen Mary* upon her launch by the King and Queen on 26 September 1934.

A ship of superlatives, *Queen Mary* was 1,019 × 118ft and 80,774 GRT. Her massive turbine power plant could drive her in excess of 30 knots, and her record was an average westbound crossing speed in August 1938 of 31.69 knots. This record stood until 1952.

Chad Valley colour take to pieces model showing internal decks, 1935.

RMS *Queen Mary* medal.

She carried more than 2,000 passengers in three classes along with 1,100 officers and crew.

Her interior design was more conventional than her pre-war rival *Normandie*. Spacious comfortable public rooms, the most impressive being the three-storey cabin-class dining room, sat alongside comfortable suites and cabins, which had a traditional British influence. Cunard brought out a publicity booklet, *The Ship of Beautiful Woods*, to showcase the use of veneers from across the Empire.

So, a fast record-breaking liner in a very traditional style, with a British take on streamline moderne, *Queen Mary* became a pre-war favourite with tourists, emigrants, first-class passengers and celebrities of the day. There are many images of the likes of Judy Garland, Gregory Peck and the Kennedy family on board, along with sports stars, business moguls, world leaders and their pets.

War in 1939 stopped the transatlantic passenger trade in its tracks and the *Queen Mary*, along with her running mate *Queen Elizabeth*, spent the period of conflict moving a huge volume of troops swiftly, safely and mostly secretly around the globe. Known as 'the Grey Ghost', she avoided U-boats but managed to ram and sink her escorting cruiser HMS *Curacao* off Ireland in October 1942. A total of 239 service personnel were lost and *Queen Mary* had to sail on lest she become a target for torpedoes. In July 1943 she carried a record 16,683 souls on one voyage, and Winston Churchill used her to cross to and from the US on a number of occasions using the alias Colonel Warden.

At the end of the war, *Queen Mary*, along with other Cunarders that had served the war effort, repatriated thousands of US service personnel and, from January to September 1946, war brides sailing to new lives in the New World.

Post-war, *Queen Mary* and *Queen Elizabeth* were refitted and ran the tandem Atlantic service for which they were designed, profitably, for many years. The end was in sight, however, with the first commercial transatlantic jet flights at the end of the 1950s. She was retired in 1967 but amazingly was acquired by the City of Long Beach in California to serve as a hotel, conference centre and tourist attraction. There she resides today, having now been in this role for longer than she was in service. There is no better opportunity to visit an original liner from the golden era of transatlantic travel.

The toy makers Chad Valley were commissioned by Cunard to create the marvellous cardboard model shown. It shows in a unique way how the different decks and areas of the ship, both passenger and working spaces fit together. All of the ship's deck layouts are here, as well as cutaway sections displaying the multi-deck engine and boiler spaces. I am not aware of any other liner for which a similar model was produced.

RMS *MAURETANIA*, CIGARETTE CASE

GREAT BRITAIN, 1938

One of the loveliest-looking liners of the post-war period, RMS *Mauretania* kept alive the name of her illustrious predecessor, which left service in 1935. The new 'Maury' was built at Cammell Laird, Birkenhead, and at 35,738 GRT and 772 × 90ft she was the biggest ship built in England up to that date. She was launched on 28 July 1938 by Lady Bates, wife of the Chairman of Cunard/White Star, Sir Percy Bates.

With her two funnels she looked like a scaled-down *Queen Elizabeth* and she was designed for the transatlantic route, supplementing the two *Queens* on the run from Southampton but also to sail from London and Liverpool. Her maiden voyage on 17 June 1939 was Liverpool to New York, but the war cut short her passenger-carrying career, and she was laid up at New York and fitted with

RMS *Mauretania* cigarette case in the shape of funnel, sold on board.

Original photograph of Captain John Treasure Jones bringing RMS *Mauretania* into Southampton for the last time.

two 6in guns before sailing to Sydney to be converted into a troop transport. Her war service saw her steam more than 500,000 miles and carry around 350,000 troops.

Adolf Hitler had offered a 50,000 DM reward to any U-boat commander who sank a *Queen* liner, or indeed *Mauretania,* and she had a close call leaving Rio on 2 September 1942, when intelligence of a wolf pack intending to intercept and sink her as she left harbour was received. Using her speed and zig-zag manoeuvring, she sailed out anyway, but the risks were ever present.

After the war, she repatriated troops to Australia, New Zealand and Canada, and took war brides to the US. Returning to Cammell Laird in April 1947 for a £1.6 million refit, she resumed her transatlantic service. From 1 January 1950, Cunard/White Star became

Original photograph of RMS *Mauretania* arriving at Inverkeithing.

the Cunard Steamship Company Ltd and the White Star name vanished from the North Atlantic.

Mauretania was refitted and had air conditioning installed in December 1957. In 1962 she was painted in two-tone 'cruising green' and ran cruises to the Mediterranean or from New York to the West Indies, calling at St Thomas, Martinique, Trinidad, Curacao, Port-au-Prince and Nassau. In March 1963, the ship sailed a new New York–Cannes–Genoa–Naples service but decreasing passenger numbers inevitably spelt the end for her. On 10 November 1965, *Mauretania* arrived in Southampton at the end of her final Mediterranean cruise.

On 20 November, she left for the trip north to Inverkeithing. In command was Captain John Treasure Jones, 60. He was a hugely experienced mariner and would go on to command *Queen Elizabeth* and *Queen Mary*. He would also take *Queen Mary* on her last voyage to Long Beach in December 1967. He navigated the River Forth without tugs and brought the ship into her final harbour at 2 a.m. under her own power, the first time a ship of this size had been brought in during the hours of darkness.

The model funnel is by Asprey of London and is actually a cigarette case sold on board.

RMS *QUEEN ELIZABETH*, MODEL BELL

GREAT BRITAIN, 1938

This small bell is a model of the original Queen Elizabeth Bell which is on display at the C.Y. Tung Maritime Museum in Shanghai, China. The story of this great Cunarder and Mr Tung would become entwined, with tragic consequences.

The second of Cunard's proposed two-ship transatlantic service was born straight into the early days of the Second World War. She had been built at John Brown's yard on the Clyde and launched on 27 September 1938. At 83,673 GRT and 1,029 × 118ft, she was designed to carry 823 first-, 662 cabin- and 798 tourist-class passengers along with 1,296 crew.

She was unfinished when Churchill ordered her to sail for New York on 6 February 1940 to safeguard her from German air attacks. She sailed in secrecy, orders as to her destination only being received once she was under way. She was expected to be going to Southampton, and on the day she had been scheduled to arrive German bombers were in evidence over the port. However, with a crew of 400 and without sea trials she made her first Atlantic crossing instead.

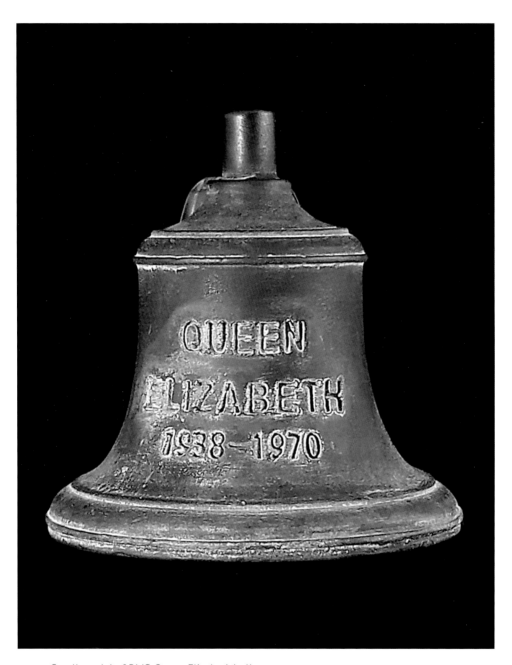

Small model of RMS *Queen Elizabeth* bell.

s.s. seawise university/**deck plan**

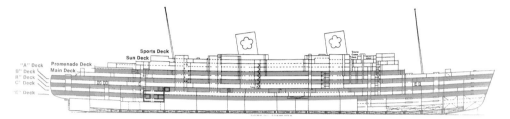

Deck plan of proposed *Seawise University* and postcard of the ship entering
New York harbour.

She spent the war trooping, along with *Queen Mary* and *Mauretania*, initially in the Far East and Australia, and from 1942 was back on the Atlantic, bringing thousands of US troops to Europe. The *Queens'* speed allowed them to sail independently of convoys as they could outrun most threats, especially U-boats.

Queen Elizabeth made her passenger-carrying maiden voyage as a liner on 16 October 1946. *Queen Mary* had been conceived in the 1930s, and had a very traditional feel, whereas changes in style and technological advances meant that, by the time she entered service, *Queen Elizabeth* had a more modern feel, and having only two funnels left more internal space. She was never quite as popular as the more conservative *Queen Mary* but the two ships ran a highly profitable service for Cunard until diminishing passenger numbers in the 1960s led to her withdrawal from service.

Initially sold to a Port Everglades company for use as a convention centre, she was sold again to Hong Kong Shipping magnate C.Y. Tung for $3.5 million. He had her sailed to Hong Kong in February 1971. Tung planned to turn the ship into a floating university and cruise liner named *Seawise University* and began an extensive refit. Her maiden Pacific cruise was set for April 1972. Around $6 million was spent on this work, which was nearly complete when fire broke out on 9 January 1972. The fire quickly consumed the ship and, in echoes of *Normandie*, huge amounts of water pumped on board by firefighters eventually capsized her.

The evidence that four fires had started simultaneously led to arson being a possible cause. There was talk of insurance fraud, or a feud between Chinese Nationalist Tung and Communist ship construction unions. The wreck was left *in situ* for a year and featured in the 1974 James Bond Film *The Man with the Golden Gun* as a British Secret Service base. Over the next two years she was broken up, but her keel and boilers remained on the seabed. They still lie there alongside the Hong Kong container terminal.

SS *LIBERTÉ*, MAIDEN VOYAGE MEDAL AND GALA RIBBON

FRANCE, 1950

The German Liner *Europa* was on a scheduled westbound crossing in August 1939 when she was ordered back to Bremerhaven owing to the imminent outbreak of war. There was talk about turning her into a landing ship for the planned invasion of Britain, and later possibly to an aircraft carrier, although neither came to pass. The end of the war found her a sorry sight, but the US pressed her into service as a troop transport, USS *Europa*.

After the end of the Second World War, many vessels that had been in use by Axis nations were taken by the Allies in recompense for losses suffered during the conflict.

Europa was transferred to the French government and moved to Cherbourg in June 1946, partly in recompense for the loss of SS *Normandie*. Her new name was *Liberté*. As was usual with

SS *Liberté* maiden voyage medal and gala ribbon.

French liners, a medal was minted to commemorate her entry into service, even though she was not technically a new build. Gala ribbons were given as souvenirs of the voyage and were available in many different colours.

Her transition back into a transatlantic liner was not to be straightforward. Having been moved to Le Havre, she broke from her moorings in a storm, ran into the wreck of the liner *Paris* and sank. Raised and taken to St Nazaire in April 1947, her conversion was further delayed by a fire in October 1949, so her maiden voyage as *Liberté* did not take place until 17 August 1950.

The French had transformed the German liner with its somewhat pre-war feel into a light and airy, very modern ship with echoes of *Normandie*. Much use was made of light European and Canadian woods, glass and imaginative lighting. There was a stunning

SS *Liberté* brochure.

first-class grand staircase and a two-storey library, as well as a winter garden and a nightclub with underfloor lighting. The French also carried out extensive strengthening of her hull and a total upgrade of firefighting and electrical systems.

With more than 1,300 passengers onboard, she left Le Havre, reaching New York on 23 August. Along with *Île De France* and *De Grasse*, *Liberté* marked the return of CGT to the North Atlantic. She was well received and many passengers who had chosen the French Line to cross pre-war rejoiced in being able to enjoy the style and service associated with their ships once again.

So began *Liberté*'s new transatlantic life. There was the odd mishap, including a grounding and a small fire, but nothing to tarnish her reputation. She even went cruising to the Caribbean in February 1952. She called at Rio, echoing *Normandie*'s famous voyages to the southern hemisphere in 1938 and 1939.

The end came in 1962 when she was sold for scrap, arriving at La Spezia, Italy, on 30 January. She had a long and varied life, launched in 1928 as the German *Europa*, seized by the US in 1945 and then having her golden years as the French *Liberté* right through the 1950s.

20

SS *UNITED STATES*
STATEROOM KEY U-183

UNITED STATES, 1952

Another survivor of the age of great ocean liners sits now on the Delaware River, Philadelphia. Although stripped of her interiors, shabby and, on the face of it, unloved, there are still people passionate about preserving her and giving her new life.

SS *United States* was conceived and built with the possibility of war in mind. The American government saw the need for a big ship that could be used as a fast troop carrier with a long range, as the world moved into an increasingly tense period post-Second World War. Designed by visionary Marine Architect William Francis Gibbs and part funded by the US government, the ship was revolutionary in her hull design, and had an immensely powerful (240,000shp) power plant. She was light for a ship of her size, her superstructure was of lightweight aluminium and she was highly

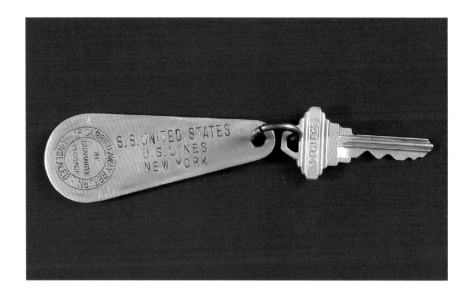

SS *United States* stateroom key.

compartmentalised, with two totally separate engine rooms. Her hull design and details of her power plant were kept secret for many years, but her power to weight ratio was incredible.

Her cruising speed would be an amazing 35 knots, but she did 43 on her trials, this for a ship 900 × 101.7ft and 53,329 tons. Imagine something the size of a skyscraper moving along at 50mph! She could even travel in reverse at over 20 knots. Not surprisingly, she snatched the Blue Riband on her maiden voyage on 3 July 1952. Her time from the Ambrose Lightship to Bishop Rock was an astounding three days, twelve hours and twelve minutes, averaging 34.51 knots. Nearly sixty years on, she still holds the record for a passenger liner.

Designed to carry 871 first-, 508 cabin- and 549 tourist-class passengers, with 1,093 crew, *United States* was also capable of being quickly converted into a 15,000-capacity troopship. Remembering the fate of SS *Normandie* lost to fire while being converted in 1942, the ship had no wood on board, except supposedly the butcher's block and some elements of the ship's pianos. Her interiors were modern, comfortable and the total opposite of the pre-war 'country house'-style liners. She soon attracted the crème de la crème of transatlantic passengers, including Salvador Dali and John Wayne. When the Duke and Duchess of Windsor began to travel on her in 1953, United States Lines immediately saw increased bookings.

Laid up in November 1969 owing to the downturn in trade caused by the rise of affordable transatlantic jet travel, she changed ownership several times, and in 1992 she was towed to Odessa to be stripped of the huge amounts of asbestos used in her construction. Stripped bare, she returned to Philadelphia, where she was acquired by Norwegian Cruise Line. The plan to put her back into service fell though owing to the huge costs involved and in February 2010 she was acquired by the SS United States Conservancy, under the chairmanship of Susan Gibbs, the granddaughter of the original designer. They work to raise funds to preserve and repurpose this iconic ship; visit www.ssusc.org to find out more.

Cabin U-183, which this key opened, was an en-suite room, situated aft on the Upper Deck, where many of the first-class cabins were located. The cabin is long gone, but the ship lives on in many hearts.

21

ANDREA DORIA, SALVAGED CURRENCY

ITALY, 1953

Before the Second World War, the Italian Line enjoyed a period of great prosperity, running gorgeous liners such as *Rex* and *Conti di Savoia*. Post-war, the fleet had been all but decimated and it was not until 1949 that the keel was laid for a true symbol of renaissance, SS *Andrea Doria*. She was to have a sister ship, *Cristoforo Colombo*.

The liner was named after the famous Genoese admiral (1466–1560), and was launched on 16 June 1951. She was built for beauty and style over size and speed. Italy's greatest artists and designers came together to create a ship that fully embodied *la dolce vita*. Elegant rather than grand, the artwork onboard was valued at $1 million and there was a life-size statue of Admiral Andrea Doria in the first-class lounge.

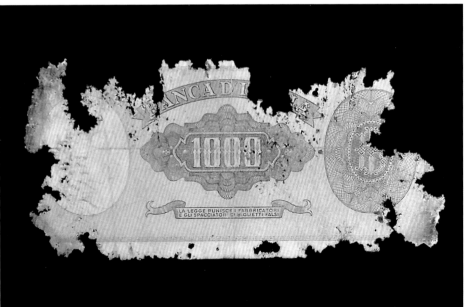

Banknote raised from *Andrea Doria* in 1981.

Above and opposite: Extracts from the original *Andrea Doria* brochure.

Carrying 1,241 passengers in three classes and with a crew of 580, *Andrea Doria*, at 697 × 90ft and around 30,000 tons, was a ship that was designed to comfortably cross the Atlantic and also to visit warmer destinations. She had three outdoor pools, one for each class, and was fully air conditioned.

Her maiden voyage from Genoa to New York started on 14 January 1953 and she arrived at Pier 54, New York, on the 23rd. She was opened to the public for $1 admission before leaving for a cruise to the West Indies. Her last voyage ended on Wednesday, 25 July 1956, near the end of her fifty-first crossing to New York. Shortly after passing the Nantucket lightship on approach to New York, she was hit on the starboard side by the Swedish America liner *Stockholm*. *Andrea Doria* had been in fog for some while but both ships had been aware of each other on radar as they converged. The collision occurred in spite of this.

Andrea Doria started to list to such an extent that many of the port lifeboats could not be launched. *Stockholm* pulled away but managed to stay afloat and took on more than 500 passengers from *Andrea Doria* via lifeboat. One lucky survivor from the *Doria* was found among the wreckage on *Stockholm*'s bow, having been plucked from her own bunk and deposited on the *Stockholm*. Many were killed by the impact, however. Other ships appeared in answer *to Doria*'s SOS, including the French Line's *Île De France*.

In all, forty-seven from *Andrea Doria* lost their lives, and five from *Stockholm*. The *Andrea Doria* turned over and sank on the afternoon of the 26th and images were captured by the world's press as she vanished in 240ft of water. Navigation officers from both ships were censured. The *Doria* was deemed to be travelling too fast in fog, while errors were been made reading the radar on the *Stockholm*.

The wreck is a difficult, dangerous dive, and more than twenty lives have been lost since she sank. Diver Peter Gimbel and his wife Elga Anderson launched 'The Doria Project' in 1981, managing to raise numerous objects including the ship's bank safe. The illustration shows a note recovered from this safe, which was opened on 16 August 1984 in a live TV broadcast.

Fact: Amazingly the SS *Stockholm* was still sailing in 2020 as *Astoria* for British cruise line CMV.

22

SS *CANBERRA*,
SOUVENIR PAINTED LIFE RING

On 20 December 1956, the P&O Line placed an order with Harland and Wolff of Belfast to construct a new liner for the UK/Australia service. The result was to be one of the most popular and striking liners of the twentieth century.

SS *Canberra*, named after Australia's capital city, was a turbo-electric liner, with steam driving turbines that generated electricity to power the engines, the same as was fitted to the *Normandie*. At 820 × 123ft and 45,000 GRT, she was the biggest liner P&O had operated to that point. Launched on 16 March 1960, she left for her maiden voyage on 2 June 1961. As often occurs with maiden voyages, however, difficulties can arise in a new ship untested in operation. Engine problems left her thirty-one hours late reaching Fremantle, Australia, but her welcome in all of the ports en route

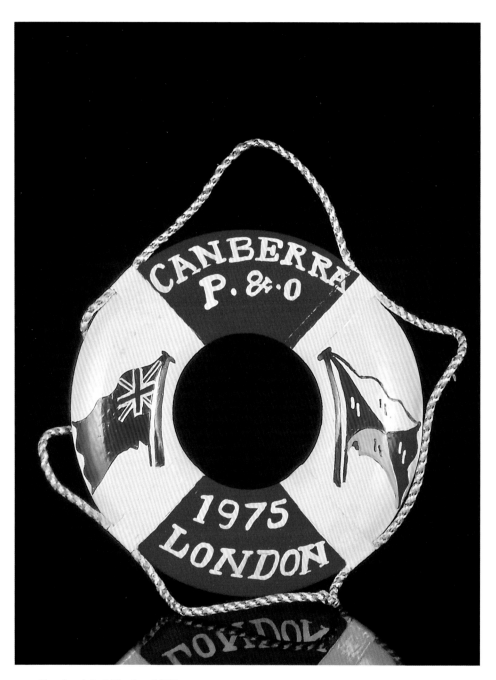

Hand-painted life ring, 1975.

was rapturous, thousands turning out to see her. She went on to Melbourne, Sydney, New Zealand, Hawaii and Canada.

Technical problems were to continue as she settled into regular service. *Canberra* also went cruising to the Mediterranean, which was a success, her huge lido areas and pools making her well suited for this role, and she ran the cruises alongside her Australia voyages. However, as passenger numbers for the Australia run diminished towards the late 1960s, mainly owing to jet travel, Canberra's future looked uncertain. P&O sent her to cruise from New York to the Caribbean but this was a dramatic failure, and there were serious plans to sell her for scrap.

Cruising, however, was becoming more popular as the seventies began, and converted to a one class cruise liner, *Canberra* found a second lease of life. She ran two- and three-week cruises from Southampton, and a popular three-month world cruise.

As the 1980s dawned, she was still successful and profitable, when she was ordered home during a Mediterranean cruise. Argentine forces had occupied the British Falkland Islands on 2 April 1982, and a task force was to be sent to confront them. On arriving at Southampton it took just three days to convert her to a troopship, including the installation of a helipad.

Two thousand troops of 40 Commando; 42 Commando Royal Marines; and 3rd Battalion, the Parachute Regiment, embarked along with stores supplies and weaponry. During the 9,000-mile voyage the troops trained, drilled and learned about the islands to which they were sailing. *Canberra* acquired the affectionate nickname 'The Great White Whale'. She survived the conflict, having sailed right into San Carlos Water, transhipping and landing troops and then transporting captured Argentine prisoners back to Argentina, before returning home to Southampton on 11 July 1982. Her welcome was rapturous, and her hull showed the ravages of her amazing endeavours in the South Atlantic.

THE POOL Most people will go far for their sunshine and their swimming, but in CANBERRA the sun and the fun are with you all the way. Step out of the Bonito Club on to the terraces surrounding a tiled pool . . . take a leisurely dip or simply laze on one of the sunbathing terraces. In a ship like CANBERRA travel is not a means to pleasure, but a sun-tanned pleasure in itself.

Inaugural brochure extract.

Refitted and returned to service, she enjoyed a renaissance, sailing until 1997 when, as with so many ageing liners, she became uneconomical to run and maintain. She sailed for Pakistan and scrapping in October that year.

The hand-painted life ring shown was available to buy on P&O and other liners. They were often painted by members of the deck crew, and could be produced as a souvenir of a voyage or an entire cruise, with the ports of call shown. Each was totally unique.

SS *FRANCE/NORWAY*, SALVAGED NAMEPLATE

FRANCE, 1960

By the time the world began to recover from the Second World War, the liners operating on the Atlantic and beyond were showing their age. Many, such as *Queen Mary* and *Île De France*, were put in service in the 1920s and '30s, while *Aquitania* had been in service since 1914! After war service, trooping and repatriating, these liners and many others were refitted for post-war service. There was no denying that they were well into middle age, or well beyond.

The French government wanted a new liner to replace *Normandie* and reinstate the glory of 'France afloat'. Having built the smaller post-war liner *Flandre*, planning started for a new CGT super liner, with President Charles de Gaulle being a strong advocate.

The 66,348 GRT, 1,035 × 110.5ft liner was launched at Penhoet, St Nazaire, on 11 May 1960 by de Gaulle's wife. *France* could carry more

Salvaged SS *Norway* nameplate from her hull. *Courtesy Trinity Marine, Devon*

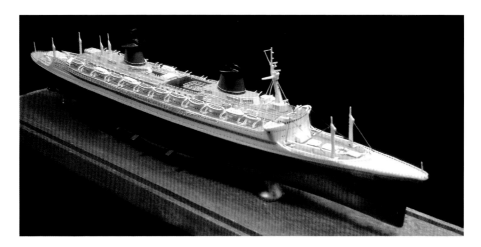

Model of SS *France* by Classic Ship Collection.

than 2,000 passengers in two classes and a crew of more than 1,200, and sailed for New York on her maiden voyage on 3 February 1962. Her interiors were certainly contemporary, with liberal use of new materials and not one piece of wood. She was described as elegant and stylish by some. Others, who remembered the pre-war extravagance of the *Normandie*, were less impressed, but times were changing.

By the early 1970s, as we have seen with many other liners, the jet age meant that liner operators had to embrace cruising and *France* undertook her first world cruise between 5 January and 2 April 1972, with 1,068 passengers. She conducted another 'Tour du Monde' from 4 January to 3 April 1974. However, unlike rivals such as the Italian Line's *Rex*, the *France* did not have a generous amount of deck or lido space and no open-air pools.

As fuel prices rose, the French government withdrew their subsidising of the ship and in September 1974 the crew went on strike demanding her continued service. The crew actually occupied the ship but to no avail, as *France* was laid up at Le Havre that December. There she remained until June 1979, when she was sold for $18 million to Norwegian NCL and was totally refitted as a cruise ship. To be more economical, only two of her four screws would operate and she was fitted with bow thrusters. Now named *Norway*, she sported a new blue and white livery.

With new deluxe suites and pools, she was a success in her new role, cruising from New York to the Caribbean, around northern Europe and the Mediterranean. However, after the terrorist attacks of 9/11, global travel declined. *Norway* also suffered a boiler room explosion in Miami on 25 May 2003, which killed eight crew and injured nineteen.

There was no coming back from this. Laid up at Bremerhaven, she was sold to Bangladeshi scrappers and after many delays, the *Norway*, now known as 'the Blue Lady', arrived at Alang and dismantling began in September 2007. By early 2009 she was gone.

The firm Trinity Marine, based in Devon, UK, oversaw the salvage of items from the ship and the huge name plates and other fittings are still in their possession.

QUEEN ELIZABETH 2,
PAINTING BY PHILIPPE CONRAD

GREAT BRITAIN, 1969

If ever there was an iconic liner, *QE2* has to be a strong contender. Launched at John Brown and Co. on Clydebank on 20 September 1967, she was to sail for Cunard until November 2008, travelling 5.5 million miles in her long career, the longest of any Cunarder.

As designed in 1965, she was to replace the two original *Queens* but also bridge the gap between a transatlantic liner and cruise ship, to enable that flexibility to make her viable in what was now the jet age. At 68,863 GRT and 963 × 105ft, she was smaller than *Mary* and *Elizabeth*, but these liners were now losing huge amounts of money for Cunard and transatlantic passenger traffic had dropped from 1 million to 650,000 passengers between 1957 and 1965. The new *Queen* would be make or break for Cunard.

An original painting of *QE2* at sea by Philippe Conrad.

The new ship was lighter than previous *Queens*, as aluminium was used in the construction of her superstructure. She was oil-fired and turbine-driven with twin screws, and much more economical than the older ships. The photograph shows a turbine blade removed during the 1986/87 refit, when she had a new diesel electric power plant installed. Thousands of these blades in differing sizes were fixed to rotors, the whole assembly housed in a casing. High-

pressure steam from the oil boilers was introduced into the casing, turning the turbines at high speed. Gearboxes transferred the power of the rotors to the propellers. As launched, *QE2* was in every way a steamship, although her original power plant was to give trouble right from her first voyage.

As a two-class ship, she would be cheaper to run than the previous *Queens* and easily adapted to a one-class format when she went cruising. Her interior design combined traditional Cunard sensibilities such as the Grills Restaurants together with a 1960s 'space age' feel, notably in the

Turbine blade removed during 1986/87 refit.

midships lobby and huge Queens Room, with its moulded white columns and illuminated ceiling. The lido decks, with indoor and outdoor pools, were ideal for cruising.

Her maiden voyage under Commodore W. Warwick took place on 2 May 1969, reaching New York after four days, sixteen hours and thirty-five minutes. As well as winter cruises, she also undertook world cruises and in 1975 her first such voyage took in twenty-eight ports over ninety-two days covering more than 32,000 miles. Over her career she completed 801 transatlantic crossings. In 1986, she was requisitioned as part of the Falklands Task Force, and took 3,000 troops of the 5th Infantry Brigade to South Georgia. Some 650 Cunard crew volunteered to go too.

On her return she was refitted and briefly painted in a light grey livery, an unpopular move that was soon changed. Her ongoing career saw further refits and an encounter with a 90ft wave. By 2004 she was cruising full time and the transatlantic service transferred to the new Queen Mary 2.

Her final voyage was Southampton to Dubai on 11 November 2008. She had been purchased for use as a floating hotel. Finally, after extensive refurbishment she opened as the QE2 Hotel at the Mina Rashid Marina, Dubai on 18 April 2018. Like her predecessor, Queen Mary, QE2 lives on. Long may she do so.

The main image shows QE2 at high speed on an Atlantic crossing. Painted by marine artist Phillipe Conrad, the picture captures the ship early in her career, conveying what was, in 1969, a radical departure in design from earlier liners. Note the high somewhat spindly funnel, which was shortened and altered in shape later in her career.

25

QUEEN MARY 2, MARITIME REPLICAS MODEL

GREAT BRITAIN, 2004

The last Atlantic liner?

The keel of Cunard's new liner was laid down at St Nazaire on 4 July 2002. The highly detailed model opposite is over 3 feet in length and clearly shows the lines and fantastic design of this modern ocean liner

Designed to replace the ageing *QE2*, the new ship weighed in at 149,215 GRT and 1,132 × 135ft. Accommodation, arranged over twelve decks, was designed in the usual Cunard fashion, with Britannia Class accommodating the majority of passengers, with its stunning two-storey dining room, and the grill classes, Princes and Queens, with suites and dedicated dining rooms and lounges.

The ship was designed by Stephen Payne OBE, Carnival Cruises' hugely experienced designer. Involved in the conception and

RMS *Queen Mary 2* model by Maritime Replicas. Scale 1/350. An identical model is on display on board.

creation of many huge cruise ships, Payne was tasked to create this, the largest ocean liner ever to sail. Far costlier (around $800 million), than a cruise ship, the financial aspect of the project almost stalled construction.

Unlike a cruise ship, built almost as a box to accommodate as many passengers as possible, *Queen Mary 2* needed a more tapered profile to enable her to move swiftly through sea conditions that would make a cruiser more than a little uncomfortable. This design, of course, made it a challenge to install the huge volume of necessary passenger and working space in a more streamlined hull. Careful design allowed around 80 per cent of staterooms to have balconies, and the ship incorporates a theatre, spa, swimming pools, numerous restaurants bars and lounges. There is the traditional Cunard Golden Lion pub, and a multi-deck atrium, the 'town square' of the ship. It is also possible to take your dog, cat or even ferret on board, with dedicated kennels and stewards.

Obverse and reverse of medal made from first cut steel from *QM2* build, July 2002.

Powered by diesel engines linked to electric Azipod motors beneath the hull, there are two further gas turbines behind the funnel providing supplemental power. Far faster than a normal cruise ship, *QM2* can attain around 30 knots, though rarely needs to. Bow thrusters and directional Azipods make her very manoeuvrable.

Looking at the ship's exterior, it is clear that there are features reminiscent of liners of the past. The curved front of the superstructure has echoes of the original *Queen Mary*. The breakwater forward has echoes of *Normandie*, while the bridge mast and funnel nod to *QE2*. This is no accident; more than a century of ocean liner evolution left a huge heritage for Payne to draw on. More than a casual glance at this *Queen* shows her to be far more than a normal cruise ship.

Constructed in sections, the ship was floated out of dock on 21 March 2003 and on 12 January 2004 she left Southampton for her maiden transatlantic crossing. The traditional pattern of summer transatlantic crossing and winter cruises continues. On 27 May 2016 the ship underwent a twenty-one-day refit, or 'remastering', of both hotel areas and technical systems, which should see her carry out her role for many years to come.

To answer the question at the start of this chapter, 'The last Atlantic Liner?', *QM2* is incredibly popular and well loved, offering the type of voyage, a 'line' voyage, that is now unique. The famous Cunard slogan of the 1950s 'Getting there is half the fun' still holds true and as long as there is an appetite for a more refined kind of travel, and a real voyage experience, there will be a place for the ocean liner.

FLAGS AND FUNNELS, OGDEN'S CIGARETTE CARDS

In the nineteenth and early twentieth centuries, tobacco firms would put collectable cards in their packaging. This allowed collectors of all ages to build a complete set of up to fifty cards, and would have driven sales as children pestered their parents or older siblings to buy the brand of tobacco that had their preferred set of cards.

Ogden's Tobacco of Liverpool was founded in 1860 and, along with other companies, they included collectable cards in their packs. In 1906, Ogden's produced this set of 'Flags and Funnels of Leading Steamship Lines'. Most of the lines shown have long gone out of business or merged with other companies, but you may recognise some.

Ogden's Flags and Funnels of Leading Steamship Lines 1906.

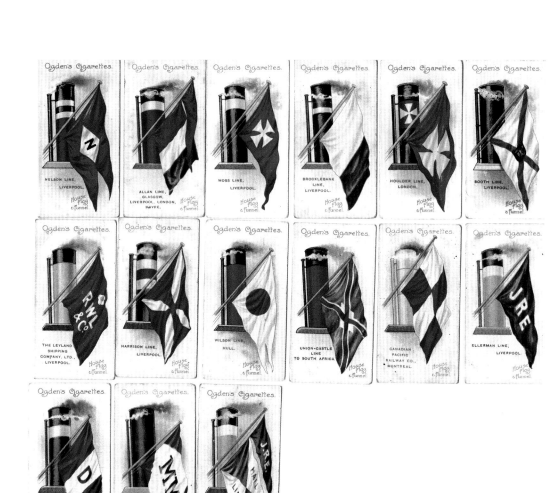

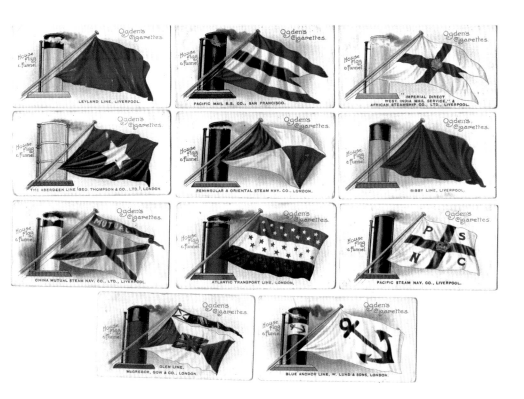

FURNESS, WITHY & CO., LTD., WEST HARTLEPOOL.

NEW ZEALAND SHIPPING CO., LTD., LONDON.

DOMINION LINE, LIVERPOOL.

ANCHOR LINE, GLASGOW.

HAMBURG-AMERICAN LINE, HAMBURG.

LAMPORT & HOLT LINE, LIVERPOOL.

AMERICAN LINE, SOUTHAMPTON—NEW YORK SERVICE.

AUSTRIAN LLOYD'S STEAM NAV. CO., TRIESTE.

WHITE STAR LINE, LIVERPOOL.

ORIENT-ROYAL MAIL LINE OF STEAMERS BETWEEN
ENGLAND AND AUSTRALIA.

BULLARD, KING & CO., NATAL LINE, LONDON.

W? JOHNSTON & CO., LTD., LIVERPOOL.

27

RMS *RAWALPINDI*, PAINTING BY NORMAN WILKINSON

THE ULTIMATE SACRIFICE

'We'll fight them both, they'll sink us, and that will be that. Good-Bye'.

These words were spoken on the bridge of the armed merchant cruiser HMS *Rawalpindi* by Captain Edward Coverley Kennedy RN. It was the afternoon of 23 November 1939, in the chill waters north of Faroe. In half an hour, Kennedy and most of the ship's crew would be dead.

Launched on 26 March 1925 at Harland and Wolff, Belfast, for P&O, the 16,619 GRT *Rawalpindi* was named after the city, which is now in the Punjab province of Pakistan. She was designed as a two-class liner for service between London and Bombay. Able to carry around 600 passengers and 380 crew, she was also fitted with

RMS *Rawalpindi*, original painting. Norman Wilkinson 1940. © P&O Heritage Collection, www.poheritage.com

refrigerated storage space. A twin-screw vessel with twin quadruple expansion engines, she could make 17 knots. Not a greyhound, she was comfortably fitted and equipped for the long journey east and back to London via the Suez Canal.

After fourteen years' service, *Rawalpindi* was requisitioned by the Admiralty for use as an armed merchant cruiser and in August 1939 she entered the Royal Albert Dock and was fitted with eight 6in and two 3in guns as well as having her aft funnel removed. She then sailed north to carry out convoy protection duties, now called HMS *Rawalpindi*. In command was 60-year-old Captain Kennedy, a vastly experienced Merchant Marine officer who had been called out of retirement. Many of the crew were P&O men who stayed on as Royal Naval Reservists and there were 276 aboard.

Souvenir bowl sold on board.

On that fateful afternoon, at 1530 a ship was sighted off to starboard. Knowing that an enemy cruiser might be in the vicinity, *Rawalpindi* headed for a fog bank to find cover. Shots were fired across her bow and orders flashed from the German ship, now identified as *Scharnhorst*, to heave to. Ignoring the order, and now at action stations, Kennedy tried to steer his ship towards an iceberg about 4 miles away in order to find cover and protection. More 'heave-to' orders came from *Scharnhorst* and more warning shots were fired. Then a bad situation became a catastrophe:

Scharnhorst's sister ship *Gneisenau* was sighted and Kennedy knew the end was near.

Refusing to surrender, *Rawalpindi* opened fire on the vastly better armed, faster armoured cruisers, scoring a hit on *Scharnhorst*. The battle lasted barely fifteen minutes. Caught in the crossfire between the cruisers, *Rawalpindi* was soon reduced to a burning wreck. In a day of heroism and in the face of certain destruction, there were individual acts of bravery on the doomed liner, as men struggled to keep individual guns firing, all central fire control having been knocked out.

The end came at 1600 when a shell from *Scharnhorst* ignited *Rawalpindi*'s forward magazine and in the tremendous resulting explosion, she broke in two and sank. There were only thirty-eight survivors. Kennedy was among the lost.

Scharnhorst was sunk off the North Cape in December 1943, caught by British battleships and cruisers. *Gneisenau* survived until being sunk as a block ship at Gotenhafen (now Gdynia) in March 1945. She was raised and scrapped after the war.

The dramatic painting is by Norman Wilkinson CBE 1878–1971, a renowned maritime artist. Among his other works was 'Plymouth Harbour', which hung in the first-class smoking room of RMS *Titanic* and was lost with the ship.

TITANIC SURVIVOR, JACK THAYER'S ACCOUNT

AN ACCOUNT OF THE SINKING OF *TITANIC* BY PASSENGER JACK THAYER. PUBLISHED 1940

This original account, signed and limited to just 500 copies, was written by John Borland 'Jack' Thayer. Jack was 17 and travelling back from a European trip with his parents, John Borland Thayer and Marian Longstreth Morris Thayer, and her maid, Margaret Fleming. The family were part of Philadelphia high society, Thayer Senior being second vice-president of the Philadelphia Railroad. Jack was travelling first class in stateroom C-70; his parents had an adjoining interconnecting cabin, C-68.

Jack's future was planned out: Princeton University, then a career in banking. During the trip, the family rubbed shoulders with the elite on board including J. Bruce Ismay, chairman of White Star,

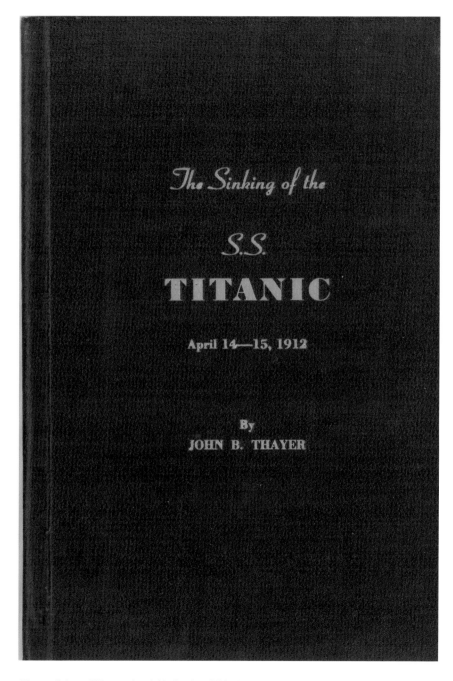

First edition of Thayer book limited to 500 signed copies.

FIRST EDITION

LIMITED TO FIVE HUNDRED COPIES.

THIS IS COPY NUMBER *113*

Surviving members of *Titanic* crew in New York. Original press photograph.

who showed them a telegram he had regarding ice ahead of the ship, though not to be reached until around 9 p.m. that night, 14 April.

Jack dined alone and later went to the deserted boat deck and noticed the brightness of the stars, the millpond-like sea, and the cold. Going to his stateroom, he opened the porthole halfway, and was just getting into bed at 11.45 when he felt the ship veer, the engines stop, start again briefly, then stop again. Jack put an overcoat on over his pyjamas and went on deck, and he was shortly joined by his father. They noticed *Titanic* listing to port, the noise of the funnels venting steam, and saw both Thomas Andrews, *Titanic*'s designer, and J. Bruce Ismay. Andrews told them that he didn't give the ship much more than an hour to live.

Hurrying below, father and son dressed, and brought Mrs Thayer and her maid to the lounge on A Deck. Jack's friend, Milton Long, whom he had met earlier, joined them. The band was by now playing lively tunes but by 12.45 rockets were being fired and Mrs Thayer and her maid moved towards the port-side boats while Jack and his father went to starboard. Discovering that the women had not found a boat, the men went with them but Jack became separated in the crowd. He never saw his father again.

By 1.25 a.m. the stern lifeboats were gone and the band was still playing, although they now wore life jackets. By 1.50, the only boats left were the collapsible type forward under the supervision of Second Officer Lightoller. Jack and Milton Long stood by the rail alongside the second funnel and as the ship began her final moments, they jumped into the freezing sea. Jack was nearly hit by a collapsing funnel, but reached an upturned boat and lived. Milton Long was never seen again. Jack watched *Titanic* disappear and described the horror of the sounds and sights of the sinking. He was one of the few witnesses to say that she might have buckled or broken as she went down.

Jack spent the night on Collapsible B until picked up by the Cunard liner *Carpathia* the next morning, being reunited with his mother, who survived along with her maid. His father had not survived. On board, Jack visited Ismay in his cabin. He was in shock, shaking and staring straight ahead, and would not even acknowledge Jack. His hair had, according to Jack's memoir, turned white.

Jack married in 1917. He and his wife had three sons. One died a few days after being born and they lost another son, Edward, in the Second World War. Jack committed suicide on 20 September 1945. He leaves us a compelling legacy in his description of events on the night of 14/15 April 1912.

AGROUND, RMS *CHINA*'S EVACUATION PHOTOGRAPHS

RMS *CHINA* P&O LINER AGROUND NEAR ADEN, 1898

This is a rarely seen photograph of an ocean liner aground and her passengers being evacuated on to a nearby rocky shore. The location is near the island of Perim at the entrance to the Red Sea near Aden. The ship is the P&O liner RMS *China*.

The 7,899-ton RMS *China* was launched in 1896 for the London to Australia service. Some 500ft long, she had capacity for 320 first- and 160 second-class passengers. Her handsome accommodation included an 80ft grand saloon, music room and 400ft promenade deck. She was powered by triple expansion steam engines.

China left Melbourne for London on 1 March under the command of Captain de Horne and she carried a cargo including wool, leather, tin, copper, lead, wine, apples and wheat. Calling at Adelaide on the 3rd and Albany on the 6th, her next call would

Original photos of RMS *China* aground, with passengers disembarking.

Silver plate butter dish as sold in RMS *China*'s Barber Shop.

be Colombo. The trip was smooth and passengers enjoyed various sports competitions, smoking room concerts and good food and company. The equator was crossed on the 14th with King Neptune coming aboard to ceremonially 'dip' those crossing for the first time. Colombo was reached and then on to Aden, where the mail from Bombay was loaded, and from where the voyage continued on Thursday, 24 March.

At 8.15 p.m., as dinner was coming to an end, there was a grinding impact as the ship came hard aground on the Azalea Rock. There was no initial panic and the band started to play. Rockets were launched and soon an evacuation began by boat to the nearby shore. Lighting was rigged to the side of the ship and by 3 a.m. all passengers were on dry land. Stewards brought supplies ashore and in the morning an overland walk to the port of Perim was undertaken, where to everyone's delight, P&O steamer *Carthage* was waiting, having been dispatched from Aden.

In this way, the passengers and crew were able to safely continue from Perim on the 27th, reaching Plymouth on 11 April and London on the 13th.

The Admiralty Court of Aden found that Captain de Horne was responsible for the wreck and he was suspended for six months. A passenger on deck reported that the ship appeared to be heading straight for the Azalea Rock, which lies to the east of a narrow passage between the island of Perim and the mainland. He stated that the engines were reversed at the last moment but to no avail, and *China* struck head on.

It took two years to refloat, repair and put RMS *China* back into service. Her repairs were done by Harland and Wolff, where her forepart was virtually rebuilt. She was put back in service on the India run. In the First World War she served as a hospital ship and survived the war, returning to commercial service before being scrapped in Japan in 1928.

30

LEST WE FORGET,
LUSITANIA PROPAGANDA

POSTER PROMOTING SALE OF LUSITANIA MEDALS.

After the loss of RMS *Lusitania*, a propaganda war began.

Shortly after the sinking, Germany minted a commemorative medal designed by Karl Goetz to commemorate their 'Great Victory' and mock the Allies for ignoring German warnings that cost them *Lusitania*. The medal depicts Death shown as a skeleton selling tickets on one side with the words 'Business Above Everything', and the sinking liner loaded with munitions on the other. However, there was worldwide condemnation at the loss of civilian life, and the German medal was to be turned to the Allies' advantage.

In a propaganda response, the British copied the medal and sold 300,000 at a shilling each, in aid of the St Dunstan's Blinded Soldiers and Sailors Hostels and the Red Cross. The image is of an original advertising poster for the medals. It shows a dramatic rendering of the sinking liner as well as images of the medal, under the heading 'Lest We Forget'.

Lest We Forget picture produced as propaganda piece to advertise *Lusitania* medals.

The loss of the ship was used to help recruit troops for the front, and there were many posters and advertisements showing the sinking *Lusitania* with proclamations such as 'Avenge the Lusitania' and 'Take up the Sword of Justice'.

Lusitania was initially left in peace, in 305ft of water 11 miles south of the Old Head of Kinsale, Ireland. Then, in the 1930s, the wreck was rediscovered and dived on by American divers, although they did not salvage anything. Over subsequent years there was talk of the Royal Navy depth charging the wreck, possibly to conceal evidence of an illicit cargo of munitions. The wreck was acquired jointly by American businessman Gregg Bemis and Partners in 1968, and Bemis took sole ownership in 1982.

An expedition was undertaken in July to August 1993 by renowned oceanographer Dr Robert Ballard. He found the *Titanic* wreck in 1985 and is famous for his other expeditions, including the German battleship *Bismarck*. Evidence of ammunition being on the wreck was there to see, but these were rifle cartridges and percussion fuses, not explosive enough to cause the massive secondary explosion. Ballard concluded that the explosion was due to the ignition of coal dust in the ship's bunkers. These 'dust explosions' can be powerful, but do generally need dry conditions. Possibly the ingress of huge amounts of cold seawater into *Lusitania*'s high-pressure power plant could have triggered the second catastrophic blast. Whatever the cause, Walter Schweiger, captain of *U-20*, maintained he only fired one torpedo.

The *Lusitania* disintegrates further year on year. Unlike *Titanic*, she is at the whim of tides, strong currents and damage by fishing nets. Like the *Titanic*, she will not be forgotten.

31

YOUR CABIN,
SS *NORMANDIE* TELEPHONE

FRANCE, 1935

The photograph shows an original telephone from a suite aboard *Normandie*. Made of Bakelite and produced by Le Materiel Telephonique, it was presumably removed prior to her conversion and loss by fire. Most of these phones only connected to the main switchboard on the ship. This one has a call button, which may have linked it to another room in the suite as well. How things have changed from the early days of liner travel.

Cunard's first liner, the paddle steamer *Britannia*, carried Charles Dickens from Liverpool to Boston in 1842. He described his cabin as a 'profoundly preposterous box', with two bunks and a sofa. The cabin turned out to be tiny, much smaller than the Cunard literature portrayed, though it did have a porthole. During a bad storm, the cabin flooded, and he and his family were unable to stand, sit or

SS *Normandie* first-class suite telephone.

find rest in any way. The ship's cow fared better: it was slung in its own hammock!

As ships became bigger, facilities improved. By 1899, White Star Line's *Oceanic* provided spacious (for the time) first-class staterooms with windows rather than portholes, wardrobe, desk and sofa, although no private bathroom facilities. These were reserved for the exclusive 'special suites'. Second class was far better than first on older liners, with comfortable cabins, mostly four or two berth, costing around £11 for a crossing in 1911. Third class varied. On *Oceanic*, men were separated from women at each end of the ship, men accommodated in open berths forward, women and

Key fob and key to ≠stateroom 315.

married couples at least having proper rooms aft and amidships but little privacy otherwise. Cunard did not segregate their steerage and generally they all occupied the same space in the forward part of the ship in two- to eight-berth rooms. Stewards and stewardesses attended to all classes, and obviously the ratio per passenger depended on class.

By the 1920s and '30s, cabins (or 'staterooms', as they were known) had evolved beyond measure. Spacious first-class cabins often had private bathrooms. There were cabin telephones, and it was possible to call anywhere in the world while at sea. Call buttons summoned stewards, room service was available and, of course, there was electric light, heating and hot water, things a passenger could only have dreamt of a couple of decades before.

Most liners had an exclusive top tier of accommodation, the deluxe suite. On the German *Imperator* back in 1913, there were two Kaiser suites with two large bedrooms, both with en suite bathrooms, dining/breakfast room and veranda, all for $5,000 per voyage.

Perhaps the epitome of the deluxe suite was found on the French Line's *Normandie*, and the crème de la crème were the grand luxe suites named Rouen, Caen, Deauville and Trouville. These suites had bedrooms and bathrooms for three couples, as well as a cabin for servants or children, salon, private dining room and pantry. Deauville and Trouville also had private deck space overlooking the stern and the ship's wake stretching to the horizon. The suites had the best of the best: crystal by Lalique, silverware by Puiforcat and Christofle, and fine china by Limoges. If you fancied a tune you had your own baby grand piano. These suites attracted the celebrities of the day: Marlene Dietrich, Cary Grant, Walt Disney and many others, who were attracted to the exclusivity, levels of service and French style that *Normandie*'s deluxe service offered.

The key shown opened the door to a first-class outside cabin on A-Deck, close to the Main Reception Hall.

32

THE STEERAGE
BY ELIZA PUTNAM HEATON

A COPY OF *THE STEERAGE*, 1888

Born in August 1860 in Danvers, Massachusetts, Eliza Putnam Heaton became a pioneering female journalist. In 1882 she married John Langdon Heaton, later to become a member of the Pulitzer Prize Board. They wrote together for the *Brooklyn Daily Times* and later for the *New York Recorder*, where she introduced a highly successful women's section. She was one of the founders of the Women's Press Club.

In September 1888, Eliza became one of the first journalists to cross from Liverpool to New York in steerage, for the purpose of describing the experience in print. The ship she joined was the Cunard Line RMS *Aurania*, 7,269 GRT and 470 × 57ft. She was steam powered but could also carry sail. This was fortuitous, as she had broken down on her maiden voyage in June 1883, and had arrived

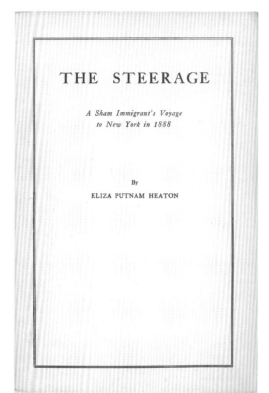

THE STEERAGE

*A Sham Immigrant's Voyage
to New York in 1888*

By
ELIZA PUTNAM HEATON

Small portrait of Eliza Putnam Heaton.

Cover of *The Steerage* by Elizabeth Putnam Heaton 1888.

at New York under sail. Broader in the beam than her predecessor *Servia*, she was known as a roller in rough weather.

Eliza acquired her steerage ticket for £4. This fare included basic provisions including three quarts of water per day, and a weekly ration by weight of bread, meat, rice, potatoes, flour, oatmeal and tea/coffee. It was forbidden for steerage passengers to buy additional food on board, although as Eliza discovered, unofficially tipping a steward could lead to 'extras' or even leftovers from cabin class. She also had to buy her own mug, plate, mattress and blanket before boarding.

She sailed from Liverpool on Saturday, 8 September and it would take ten nights to cross. Steerage was in the forward part of the ship, low down so portholes could not be opened at night or in rough weather. For steerage passengers all meals were taken in the

Steerage ticket receipt, RMS *Aurania*, 9 January 1895.

A No. 23573

CUNARD LINE.

STEERAGE OUTWARD.

Date, *January 9* 1895

For Steamer *Aurania*

To Sail *January 12* 1895

Booked to *Dublin via Queenstown*

14 20 Amount, $ XXX 60 18.00
15.00

Commission ?

Advised *January 14/95*

NAMES OF PASSENGERS.	AGES.
James Maguire	40

One Adults, *No* Child., *No* Inft.

Apl. '94—5,000

Remitted Jan 14/95

main common room, which was about 60ft long with sleeping rooms off, each housing twenty-four people in berths only 2ft wide. There was access to deck space forward, but the lavatory arrangements had to be accessed through crew areas and were woefully inadequate for the amount of passengers. After meals, one bowl of water was provided on deck for washing plates and mugs, for up to 700 emigrants!

The journey was not smooth, there being a delay at Queenstown (now Cobh) and a violent storm on the 11th/12th. Sickness was rife, with the associated unpleasantness, smell and appalling atmosphere that resulted from the enclosed space. The ship rolled and pitched horribly. There were babies and children on board, and parents, horribly sick themselves, could only hope for help from the less sick to comfort them. During the calmer periods, there was music, dancing, card playing and singing. Eliza read and learned about her fellow travellers, mostly English, Irish, Welsh, Scots and French. Most were looking for a new life, leaving the poverty of the Potteries or rural Ireland for new opportunities. There were miners, farmers and women looking to go into service.

Eliza managed to blend in and was accepted as part of steerage, although by the time New York was reached, she was weak from the diet and lack of sleep. Her account was published in various newspapers on 20 and 21 October 1888. She died in Brooklyn on January 1919, and her husband published the memoir that year as *The Steerage: A Sham Immigrant's Voyage to New York in 1888.*

Left: Cabin-class passenger list from
RMS *Aurania*, Liverpool to New York,
18 September 1886.

33

ALL ABOARD!,
SS *NORMANDIE* LIFEBOAT PLAQUE

A LIFEBOAT NAME PLAQUE FROM SS *NORMANDIE*

Of all the facilities on board a liner, the lifeboats are arguably the most important – but, on the other hand, hopefully the least likely to be used. The illustration opposite shows a lifeboat plaque from SS *Normandie*, which carried a total of fifty-six boats. These were still attached to the ship when she burned at her berth in New York while being converted to a troopship on 9 February 1942. Meanwhile, the illustration on page 158 shows an original tin of lifeboat and raft ration biscuits from RMS *Queen Mary*. These, along with fresh water, would have been aboard the boats in readiness for use should the need to evacuate the ship arise.

The ship carried twenty-four motor-driven lifeboats, each able to accommodate 145 people. Three years of experimenting and testing took place before the final design was approved. The boats were 36 × 12ft and steel built with powerful diesel engines. A full set of oars was also provided, although it was hoped that these would

SS *Normandie* lifeboat plaque and lifeboat prior to installation on board.

not be needed. Two of the boats also had radios, and two had high-speed engines for rescue purposes. The davits allowed a boat to be launched quickly by one man.

Contrast this with the lifeboats on an *Olympic*-class liner as originally built. There were fourteen clinker-built 30ft boats; two smaller emergency cutters kept ready for immediate launch; and four collapsible boats, which were more like rafts and had collaps-ible canvas sides. These could be stowed more or less flat and the sides raised to form the boat. The boats were lowered by Welin-patented davits, which allowed the boats to be swung out and

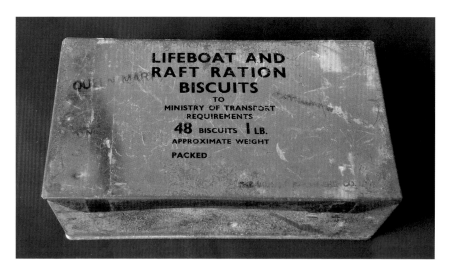

Box of biscuits from a *Queen Mary* lifeboat.

lowered, with eight to ten crew needed to do so. These davits could handle sixty-four boats but only sixteen were fitted pre-*Titanic*. The extra boats were not felt necessary under the current regulations, and further were considered to clutter the decks.

Therefore, when *Titanic* sank on 15 April 1912, she had a lifeboat capacity for only 1,178 persons, yet she carried 2,208. In fact, had she been full on her maiden voyage, she could have had more than 3,500 passengers and crew aboard. There were 3,500 lifejackets and forty-eight life rings on board but these offered no protection against immersion in the icy North Atlantic. If you weren't in a boat, or picked up by one very quickly, you died.

Travel on a cruise ship or liner today and you will have an evacuation and lifeboat drill before you sail. You won't enter a lifeboat, but you will learn what the ship's alarm signals mean, where your muster station is and how to put on a life jacket. It is very unlikely that you will ever need to evacuate your ship at sea, but rest assured that lifeboats, and indeed safety at sea, have come a long way since the days of *Titanic*.

FIRE!
SS *MORRO CASTLE* AFLAME

Of all the catastrophes that can befall a ship, fire is the most feared. It has the capacity to render the ship uninhabitable and incinerate the lifeboats as well. People can become trapped below decks, killed by smoke and fumes, or caught in the open with no escape but jumping into the sea, as flames and smoke engulf the vessel towards them.

On 6 September 1934, the Ward Line's *Morro Castle*, 11,520 GRT, caught fire off Long Island. There were strange circumstances: the ship's captain had been found dead earlier, heart attack suspected, and the first officer had taken command. Fire was reported around 3 a.m. but the ship continued steaming into a headwind, which fanned the flames. The resultant conflagration killed many trapped below decks and the rest retreated to the stern. Only six boats were

Original photograph of SS *Morro Castle* aground at Asbury Park.

launched and many were killed jumping overboard. Rescue came eventually but 135 were killed. The ship, abandoned, beached herself at Asbury Park, New Jersey, and thousands came to see the wreck before she was towed away for scrap.

On 9 February 1942, as she was being converted to a troopship in New York, the French liner *Normandie* was set alight by sparks from a welding torch igniting a stack of kapok life preservers. Like *Morro Castle*, the ship had many flammable internal components and her state-of-the-art fire protection system had been disconnected. After three hours it was thought that the fire was under control but the fire services had pumped so much water into her that she began to list and by 0245 had rolled on to her port side. There were many injuries but only one fatality.

Renamed *Lafayette*, the ship was stripped of her superstructure and the hull was eventually righted. Tragically, this amazing liner was beyond salvage and her remains were towed away for scrap.

Many items were taken off *Normandie* before conversion started, including art work, service ware, carpets and furniture. Her huge first-class dining room doors are in use in a Catholic Cathedral in Brooklyn.

Today, safety at sea, including fire protection, is covered by SOLAS, the Safety of Life at Sea convention. In the 1930s, '40s and '50s, there were alarms and extinguishers, of course. *Normandie* had a high-pressure water system with 504 hose points on board. The problem was the prevalence of wood, veneers, Formica and other combustible materials used in construction. *Queen Mary* was known as 'the Ship of Beautiful Woods' – say no more!

On a modern liner or cruise ship there will be systems to isolate fire and smoke, fire doors and segregated ventilation systems. There are sprinkler systems, often of the efficient fog or mist type that use less water but suppress fire more effectively. Of course, there are also highly trained firefighting teams who drill regularly for all kinds of threat. When you next admire that lovely wood panelling on a modern vessel, rest assured it isn't really wood.

35

LOST AND FOUND, *LUSITANIA* WATCH MECHANISM

A CASED WATCH MECHANISM SALVAGED FROM RMS *LUSITANIA* WRECK

There is a perennial fascination with shipwrecks, and none more so than the lost liner. There is sorrow and respect for those who lost their lives and a great appetite for the stories of those who survived. There is also sadness at the loss of a great ship and thoughts of what former glory may remain on the sea floor. What stories were played out on those decks and what treasures might lie within?

RMS *Titanic* was discovered by Dr Robert Ballard and his team in September 1985. She has subsequently been photographed, surveyed, videoed internally, and had her artefacts brought to the surface and displayed in travelling exhibitions. We can watch her gradual natural disintegration but also the damage caused by many submersible visits. Tourist expeditions have been advertised for

Cased watch mechanism salvaged from *Lusitania*.

in excess of $100,000. There is a line between historic and scientific exploration and conservation, and commercialism, tourism and possible plundering of a grave site. A UK/US agreement in January 2020 to protect and control access to the wreck may finally draw that line.

It took more than seventy years to find *Titanic* at great depth. When *Andrea Doria* sank off Nantucket on 26 July 1956, divers reached her the very next day and photographed the wreck. At 240ft it is a dangerous dive; in the intervening years many have made the descent and a number of lives have been lost in doing so. Many artefacts have been brought up, and china, silverware and other artefacts regularly come up for auction.

On 20 May 1922, the P&O liner *Egypt*, 7,912 GRT and 500 × 54ft, was struck by another steamer in fog off Finistère, north-west France. The ship was heading from Tilbury to Marseille and Bombay. *Egypt* sank in around twenty minutes and of 352 on board, eighty-six were lost.

Egypt was carrying in her holds more than £1 million in gold and silver bullion and coins. There were 1,089 gold bars, 1,229 silver bars and 165,979 gold coins, and not surprisingly the search for the wreck began almost immediately. She wasn't found until 1930, when an Italian salvage firm located her in 360ft of water, at the limits of contemporary diving technology. Using a patent diving apparatus resembling a one-man diving bell, it was possible to reach *Egypt*, blast open the wreck and, by lowering mechanical grabs from the salvage ship, recover almost all the valuable cargo.

The image shows a cased pocket watch mechanism brought up from the wreck of RMS *Lusitania* in 1982. This case has not been opened, but inside will be what is left of the original mechanism. The consignment, in these small brass boxes, came from the American Elgin Watch Company. The actual watch cases that have also been recovered are believed to have been manufactured by the Philadelphia Watch Company, and the two pieces of each watch were shipped separately and assembled once they reached the UK, apparently to save on duty payable on complete watches.

PASSENGER LIST, SS *CRETIC*

NEW YORK, 1912

You are about to embark on your voyage. You will be on the ship for a week, or much longer if you are travelling east to India or south to Australia. You will be sharing your leisure and meal times with a variety of companions; most, if not all, may be unknown to you. If you were in first class, your status as a business person, celebrity or world traveller meant that your social circle at sea could mean encountering familiar faces, as your peers probably travelled for the same reasons as you did, could afford luxury and used the same ships. A passenger list was essential in order to know who you knew on board; who you wanted to spend time, and be re-acquainted with; and, perhaps most importantly, who you would prefer to avoid!

The example shown is for the White Star Line SS *Cretic*, 13,517 GRT, and her voyage from Boston to Naples and Genoa departing

THE LARGEST (Triple-Screw) STEAMER IN THE WORLD.

OLYMPIC, - - - 45,324 Tons

NEW YORK–CHERBOURG–SOUTHAMPTON SERVICE

Calling at QUEENSTOWN (Westbound) and PLYMOUTH (Eastbound).

FROM SOUTHAMPTON		STEAMER.	FROM NEW YORK CALLING AT PLYMOUTH AND CHERBOURG	
DATE.	SAILING HOUR.		DATE.	SAILING HOUR.

SPECIAL NOTICE

The attention of the Managers has been called to the fact that certain persons, believed to be Professional Gamblers, are in the habit of travelling to and fro in Atlantic Steamships.

In bringing this to the knowledge of Travellers, the Managers, while not wishing in the slightest degree to interfere with the freedom of action of Patrons of the White Star Line, desire to invite their assistance in discouraging Games of Chance, as being likely to afford these individuals special opportunities for taking unfair advantage of others.

			STEAMER				
..	00	Wed.	....	OLYMPIC	..	9	Sat.
Nov. 6		Wed.	....	MAJESTIC	.. 16	Sat.	Noon
.. 13		Wed.	....	OCEANIC	.. 23	Sat.	Noon
.. 20		Wed.	....	OLYMPIC	.. 30	Sat.	Noon
.. 27		Wed.	....	MAJESTIC	Dec. 7	Sat.	Noon
Dec. 4		Wed.	....	OCEANIC	.. 14	Sat.	Noon
.. 11		Wed.	....	OLYMPIC	.. 21	Sat.	3.00 pm
.. 18		Wed.	....	MAJESTIC	.. 28	Sat.	Noon
					1913		
.. 25		Wed.	....	OCEANIC	Jan. 4	....	Noon

★ American Line Steamer

167

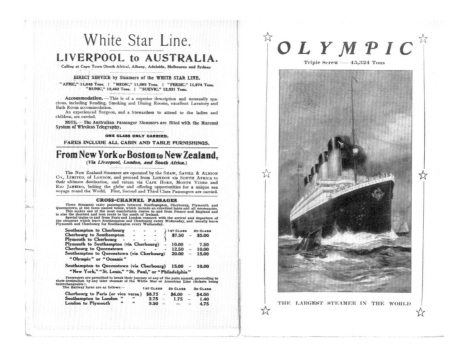

RMS *Cretic* passenger list.

Saturday, 18 May 1912. This voyage was just five weeks after the loss of RMS *Titanic*, and the list has some interesting features.

The Boston–Europe route was secondary in importance to the New York–Southampton run. There is, however, a schedule of New York sailings inside the front cover. This shows *Olympic*, and already mentions *Majestic*, which was brought out of retirement to fill the gap in the schedule left by *Titanic*. Inside the rear cover is an advertisement showing the RMS *Olympic*, tellingly now advertised as the largest steamer in the world in the absence of her slightly larger sister, now lost.

In addition to advertisements for the line, a passenger list often carried information for travellers. This could include meal-time and on-arrival baggage arrangements, as well as how to send telegrams, hire deck chairs or see the doctor on board. Above the

FIRST CLASS PASSENGER LIST
PER
S. S. "CRETIC."
COMMANDER: R. LOBEZ, LIEUT., R. N. R.

SURGEON: H. DANVERS.

PURSER: O. BARTLETT.
(*Asst. Paymaster R. N. R.*)

ITALIAN SURGEON: P. DE BLASIO.

CHIEF STEWARD: A. L. GOSLING.

TO NAPLES AND GENOA
VIA AZORES, MADEIRA, GIBRALTAR AND ALGIERS.

FROM BOSTON, SATURDAY, MAY 18, AT 11 A. M.

Andrews, Miss Kate
Atkins, Mrs. Selina

Bailey, Mr. Henry Turner
Bailey, Mrs.
Ballou, Rev. W. J.
Banigan, Mr. Joseph
Banigan, Mrs.
Bigelow, Mrs. Blanche
Bigelow, Miss Helen K.
Bishop, Miss Endora
Blodgett, Mrs. Charles W.
Blodgett, Master Emmon W.
Bobb, Mrs. P. M.
Bonner, Mrs. Samuel
Bourke, Mrs. John G.
Bourke, Miss Anna
Bourke, Miss Pauline
Brewster, Mr. William
Briggs, Mr. Richard A.
Brooks, Mrs. W. D., Jr.,
Brush, Dr. F. S.
Brush, Mrs.
Brush, Miss Charlotte
Buffington, Miss Mabel

Bunker, Mr. Charles D.
Bunker, Mrs.
Bunker, Mr. E. A.
Bunker, Mr. Thomas
Bunker, Mrs. E. A.
Bunker, Miss L.
Bunnell, Mr. M. D.
Burroughs, Miss T. M.
Bush, Miss Gladys

Carbone, Mr. Giovanni
Carbone, Mrs.
Carbone, Miss Rosalinda
Carbone, Master
Carrick, Miss Stephens
Christie, Miss Mary R.
Cobb, Mrs. Duane P.
Cobb, Master Mortimer
Coe, Miss Helen
Cowles, Mrs. Sarah E.
Cowles, Miss Nellie W.
Cragin, Miss Gertrude
Crandall, Mr. J. N.
Crandall, Mrs.
Crandall, Master Carlin
Crandall, Miss Elizabeth

list of passengers, the senior crew were listed; always the captain and often the surgeon, purser and chief steward, and sometimes chief engineer.

On boarding, the passenger list would normally be in your cabin. There would be excitement in seeing if any famous passengers were on board, although they sometimes preferred to travel incognito. Fred Astaire, Laurel and Hardy, Audrey Hepburn and Walt Disney were all regular transatlantic travellers. You might be travelling alongside Clark Gable or the Duke and Duchess of Windsor, although the latter were rarely seen, preferring to remain in their suite.

Returning to our 1912 voyage, a special notice in red print has been added:

> The attention of the Managers has been called to the fact that certain persons, believed to be Professional Gamblers, are in the habit of travelling to and fro in Atlantic Steamships.

These gamblers or card sharps were a regular feature of transatlantic travel, usually in first class. They would engage passengers who they thought were good prospects in friendly games of cards for low stakes, manage to lose convincingly until the stakes were raised high enough, then take the poor victim to the cleaners. They were active on *Titanic*, though undoubtedly under assumed names.

SELLING THE DREAM, SHIPPING LINE BROCHURES

In the pre-internet, pre-television age, selling your product was a very different challenge to today. Newspaper and magazine advertising was key, but a shipping company also had to produce promotional material, whether for a new ship or route; advertising a cruise; or, most importantly, capturing passengers who might book with one of your rivals.

Companies such as Italia, French Line and Cunard commissioned artists and designers to produce stunning posters extolling the virtues of their liners. Often, the liner was shown as a huge imposing vision, steaming full ahead, with smaller vessels, totally out of scale, dwarfed by the leviathan and its bow wave. Artists such as Charles Dixon, Cassandre, Albert Sebille and Ken Shoesmith produced amazing pieces of art. Shipping companies also commissioned original postcard art as well as using photographic images. Lund's Blue Anchor Line had hand-painted flowers on their cards, each card being totally individual.

RMS *Caronia* cutaway extract.

SS *Normandie* view over the stern, from a publicity brochure.

The brochure was another vital piece of media. Whether given out by travel agencies or from the shipping line's office, these again showed off the interiors of the liner. If it was a new ship the images might be highly stylised artist's impressions, and again the portrayal of huge scale was applied liberally and imaginatively to these interior spaces. These were, of course, the days before trade description regulation, and the artist had free reign, showing glamourous couples descending huge staircases into vast salons that no seagoing ship of the time could possibly accommodate.

Most cruise ships today will hand their guest on arrival a fold-out map of the ship, and they are certainly needed to find one's way from atrium to bar. Look then at the cutaway of Cunard's RMS *Caronia*. A relatively small liner, but look at the detail: the door opened to a hive of activity, massive engines and boilers, sumptuous cabins and salons. This is exactly what the companies were selling, and most liners have had this type of diagram published, given out by travel agencies or on board.

Once at sea you could, of course, send company-branded postcards or buy your friends and family souvenirs, dolls, models, paintings and books, all promoting in some way the ship and the line.

The French Line rather foolishly branded the ashtrays on *Normandie*'s maiden voyage with the name of the ship. On opening the ship to visitors at New York, most of these were stolen. Good advertising maybe, but the ship's name was removed from future versions.

In port, enterprising traders would brand their wares with a ship's image or name. In Le Havre, more or less any porcelain or glass pot, trinket or novelty that you can imagine was at some point embossed or painted with a French Line ship.

The legacy is that the collector of ocean liner memorabilia today has a plethora of items and ephemera to find, some of it horrendously expensive, some that can be bought for next to nothing. Beware though there are also plenty of fakes, especially White Star Line related.

THE SOUL OF A SHIP, FRENCH LINE BOOKLET

FRANCE, 1930S

In the 1930s, the French Line published this booklet, *The Soul of a Ship*, giving an illustrated and rather poetic guide to on-board personnel. I will quote from it:

> The French Line Officer – His career at sea begins at an early age, generally aboard a sailing vessel where he 'learns the ropes' by strenuous labour and much theory by arduous study. If he survives the physical and scholastic demands this period of training makes upon him, he has a long and thorough technical education, in general much the same as given to Naval Cadets, in navigation and its many kindred subjects, as well as in cargo loading, freight regulations, marine insurance and other phases of the Merchant Marine Officer's duties. His examinations satisfactorily passed, he

His labors seem light, to the casual observer, but they are exacting. Besides being a keen business executive, responsible for the comfort and satisfaction of his passengers, he is cordial, unruffled, with a sense of humor and a tolerance of human nature and its foibles. He has that rare quality, finesse, and it is his hand —his enthusiasm—that guides social activities aboard ship.

The PURSER

Extracts from *The Soul of a Ship.*

is then advanced to the grade of Student Officer aboard one of our big express liners where, under the tutelage of experienced officers, he has an opportunity to put theory into practice. Not until he has made several trips in this capacity, is he regularly commissioned a Junior Officer and then he is assigned to a small freighter. Thus, by the time he is advanced to a post on a big passenger liner, he is an experienced, capable, veteran officer. In recent years, the Student Officers of the entire French Merchant Marine have been trained aboard the French Line training-ship JACQUES CARTIER, a modern steamer of 13,000 tons.

The Captain – A man of great strength of character; a polished gentleman; a masterful commander; a perfect host to his passengers and a stern but affectionate father to his crew; his religion is the traditions of the sea. His quiet dignity inspires confidence. Veteran of many voyages, he has attained his high position only after long apprenticeship in lower grades. Such is the French Line Captain.

The Purser – His labours seem light to the casual observer, but they are exacting. Besides being a keen business executive. Responsible for the satisfaction of his passengers, he is cordial, unruffled, with a sense of humour and a tolerance of human nature and its foibles. He has that rare quality. Finesse, and it is his hand – his enthusiasm – that guides social activities aboard ship.

The Chief Engineer – He has a veteran's experience. Years of study and a wealth of technical training have made him a practical engineer, one well worthy of keeping the ship's engines fit for their important task. Their almost inaudible throbbing is to him as the pulse-beats of a patient are to the Doctor. But, where the physician ministers to his charge when health fails, the Chief Engineer ministers to his engines to keep them well.

The Chief Steward – Competent, tactful discreet; attentively courteous, but like the staff he supervises and controls, unobtrusive. If one's trip is wholly satisfying and delightful, much of the credit is his. For 'like master, like man' and he is the immediate chief of stewards and stewardesses. Want something special for luncheon? Private little dinner party? He'll fix it gladly.

The Chef de Cuisine – Unseen god of gastronomy, genius of gustatory delights, sultan of sauces, dictator of delectable, caliph of the culinary art; seldom seen, his presence is manifest by the savoury and bounteous offerings beneath which your dining table groans. He is French; a master of the fine art of cookers as the French practice it – the accepted standard with epicures throughout the world.

39

THE SOUL OF A SHIP PART 2, SS NORMANDIE CAP

This jolly looking crew cap was possibly used on board or sold as a souvenir in one of the boutiques. Continuing the French guide to personnel on a 1930s liner, I would point out that the general descriptions of roles is applicable to any contemporary shipping line:

The Doctor – A skilled professional man and an earnest reassuring practitioner; genial and gay ship's officer when his duties no longer require his attention, quiet and well qualified physician and surgeon when called upon for his expert services. And those services are freely at the disposal of passengers under his benign care twenty-four hours out of the twenty-four.

The Orchestra Leader – He is a graduate – and like as not holds a first prize-of the Paris Conservatoire, and an accomplished musician to his fingertips. In his multi-coloured garden of

French Line cap, from *Normandie*.

melody, one finds everything from the delicate rose of the classical to the gaudy sunflower of jazz. With concert music and swing rhythms he and his gifted fellow-artists contribute much to the enjoyment of your crossing.

The Wireless Operator – Way in the background of every trans-Atlantic voyage, the wireless operator stands like a shadowy sentry. Unless one wishes to have a message flashed to shore, he is hardly given a passing thought. But sea travel has been stripped of hazards by the radio-man and his apparatus. Before he attains a post aboard a French Liner, his ability has been well tested. Tenacity is strong in his make-up; he is equal to any and every eventuality.

The Stewardess – Deft, trained and courteous, she is all attention to Madame's needs – or those of Madame's precious little ones. Steward and Stewardess alike are in constant readiness to serve well and with quiet perfection. The Stewardess anticipates

Illustration from *The Soul of a Ship*.

Madame's desires and carries them out with gratifying efficiency. Instinctively, she directs her efforts towards Madame's every comfort and, possessing the valuable quality of human understanding, more than lives up to the confidence she inspires.

The Sports Director – At your service to organise or direct your physical exercise – or join you in it, if you lack a companion-at-sports. He knows all the popular deck games – shuffle board, Ping-Pong, deck tennis, and is accomplished at various sports, swimming, trap-shooting etc., and is an experienced tactful advisor, supervisor, instructor, umpire and player. And if he sees you 'overdoing it', he's only 'playing the game', if he warns you to 'take it easy'.

The Barman – His skill in mixing drinks, however great, is but one of the many qualities which make him a good barman. Long association and familiarity with his precious liquids have taught him to appreciate their virtues-and to deplore their misuse. A master of tact and diplomacy, he suggests a choice for the undecided, but discourages the too determined. Sobriety and moderation are his creed, and he always recommends them.

The Seaman – France has always been a maritime nation. Since the Phoenicians first sailed their galleys Northward across the Mediterranean, and founded what is now one of the world's greatest ports – Marseilles – the men of France have been mariners. Brittany, since time immemorial, has bred a race of hardy sailors. The history of France and the sea are one, and across its pages are spread such illustrious names as Cartier, De Grasse … Brave, faithful, intelligent and devoted to duty, the men who man the French Liners of today are of the same breed as their distinguished fo'bears.

COCKTAIL,
RMS *QUEEN MARY* DRY MARTINI

MARTINI IN CUNARD WAVE PATTERN GLASS BY STUART CRYSTAL,
AS DESIGNED FOR RMS *QUEEN MARY*

The ocean liners that sailed to and from the United States during the 1920s and early '30s were subject to the laws of prohibition. This banned the sale of alcohol and was driven by a strong Temperance Movement in the US. Brought in during January 1920 by the eighteenth amendment and repealed in December 1933 by the twenty-first amendment, US liners had to remain 'dry', while non-US ships could only open their bars outside US coastal waters. Naturally, during the period of prohibition, thirsty US passengers would book passage on a foreign vessel, and the eponymous 'booze cruise' began as a way to circumvent the regulations.

In 1930, Harry Craddock published his famous book (still in print) *The Savoy Cocktail Book*. This is the original cocktail bible and

Dry Martini in Cunard Stuart Crystal 'wave pattern' glass.

First edition of *The Savoy Cocktail Book*.

His skill in mixing drinks, however great, is but one of many qualities which make him a good barman. Long association and familiarity with his precious liquids have taught him to appreciate their virtues—and to deplore their misuse. A master of tact and diplomacy, he suggests a choice for the undecided, but discourages the too determined. Sobriety and moderation are his creed, and he always recommends them

The BARMAN

'The Barman' from the French Line's *The Soul of a Ship* booklet.

libations such as the White Lady (gin, Cointreau and lemon juice) and the Classic Dry Martini (gin and vermouth, dash of bitters) became part of the tradition of a liner voyage, along with many other recipes. A Cunard barman would learn to mix at least 300 cocktails, and on a transatlantic voyage the mix of European and US favourites exposed passengers to a whole new world of alcoholic indulgence. Americans tended to prefer cocktails, while British passengers would opt for G&T or sherry, although this changed as palates became more adventurous. A universally accepted 'pick-me-up', whether from overindulgence or sea sickness, was the Bloody Mary (vodka, tomato juice, lemon juice, tabasco and Worcester sauce, with a pinch of celery salt). On the liners of the 1930s, 'Happy Hour' stretched from the early hours of the morning to … the early hours of the morning, and ships would have their own signature cocktails. *Carmania*'s Pimm's Cup was a usual Pimm's, but with added gin!

Cocktails were often served in stunning bars or lounges. The observation bar on *Queen Mary* was a semicircular room at the front of the superstructure with a raised seating area enjoying panoramic views over the bow. There was a huge Makassar ebony-fronted bar with original murals, walnut panelling and chrome detailing. The bar is still intact on *Queen Mary* today and a highlight of any visit. This room is echoed on the current Cunard *Queens* with their elegant bow-facing Commodore Club bars. On *Normandie*, apart from numerous bars and lounges, the first-class café-grill opened on to the terraced rear decks. This room functioned as a premium restaurant, but after dining had finished, the chrome and green leather chairs were cleared and a dance floor revealed. Cocktails and dancing could be enjoyed into the early hours, and a dance band would strike up after midnight.

Today, mixology is ever more popular and on-board classes can be taken on Cunard liners. Retiring then to the nearest bar, drinks named after famous captains are available. The Commodore Sir Edgar Britten has a mix of cognac, ginger liqueur and black treacle. The list encompasses the classic Martini and its variations; dirty, French, Vespa, etc. There are classic Negronis, Daiquiris, Old Fashioned, and even a cocktail containing squid ink, which tastes much nicer than it sounds!

Cunard commissioned Stuart Crystal to produce special 'wave pattern' stemware for use on *Queen Mary*, and it was subsequently used across the fleet. The Dry Martini shown is in one of these glasses.

41

SOUVENIRS,
SS *GIULIO CESARE* PAINTING

The main image is a small picture in a gilt frame and is actually a hand-painted rendering of the Italian Line's *Giulio Cesare*, 27,000 GRT. Painted on celluloid, this is a classic view showing the streamlined liner at speed. This picture was purchased in the on-board boutique and was one of the more upmarket souvenirs available.

The second image shows an EPNS bud vase from RMS *Olympic*. Souvenirs like this were often sold in the ship's barber shop in the days before dedicated on-board shops and boutiques became common. Other items on sale included dolls, often dressed as sailors; pennants branded with the ship's name or that of the shipping line; and painted model life rings, which often had a photograph or painting of the ship in the centre. Silverware such as the vase overleaf were also available, and one could buy cruet sets, small bowls, ashtrays and paperweights, all branded with the crest of the shipping line and name of the ship. These are sometimes confused

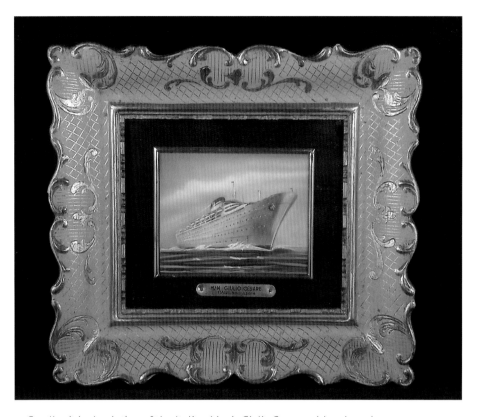

Small original painting of the Italian Line's *Giulio Cesare* sold on board.

with items from the on-board service, which may have borne the company name or crest but rarely the name of the ship, as their use could be interchangeable between vessels.

Postcards have always been a popular souvenir and were often sent to family or friends just before sailing, or posted at a port of call. Some shipping companies also provided 'arrived safely' cards, which in the days before radio or telephony could be the only way that those at home would hear that their loved ones had arrived at the end of a long and possibly perilous voyage. Most shipping companies commissioned artwork for their postcards and posters, and artists such as Charles Dixon, Ken Shoesmith and Charles Turner

became prolific in their output. The original paintings and indeed the postcards can be highly collectable. Photographic postcards were also popular, often showing excellent views of the interiors of the ships as well. They could be bought individually or in packs showing multiple views.

Gala or 'cap tally' ribbons were often given out at special dinners or events, or on the last night of a voyage. Menus were also often kept as souvenirs of a voyage. Most ships had a printing press and menus with different designs were taken on board as blanks and then printed with the day's culinary offerings. The same went for theatre programmes, concerts and competitions such as horse racing events (not real horses, model ones). An important event or gala dinner might warrant a lavish and specially printed menu just for that one meal. Some of these items of ephemera are artworks in themselves and highly sought after by collectors.

Moving into the 1930s, ships such as *Normandie* and *Queen Mary* had shopping areas with a number of boutiques selling clothing, luxury goods such as handbags and jewellery, and perfume. Jean Patou, the French perfumer, actually created a perfume called 'Normandie' in 1935, in celebration of the liner. A glass bottle held in a metal model of the ship was available.

Overleaf: RMS *Olympic* bud vase, sold on board.

MENUS,
SS *NORMANDIE* GALA DINNER

FEBRUARY 1938

From the early days of liner travel, food was an important part of the voyage. Menus, often printed on board, offered culinary delights commensurate with class. Some of these menus are art works in themselves.

In third class or steerage on an early twentieth-century liner, many passengers experienced a quality and quantity of food that was probably far better than they had known up to that point. A menu from *Titanic*'s last day, 14 April 1912, shows four meals including a breakfast of porridge, kippers, ham and eggs, tea and coffee. Dinner would include roast beef, boiled potatoes and plum pudding. Then there was tea, comprising cold meat; cheese; pickles; stewed figs; and rice, and a supper of cabin biscuits, cheese and gruel. Many other liners still made steerage passengers pay for food on top of the fare, or bring their own.

SS *Normandie* gala dinner menu cover and interior.

However, White Star and other lines were working hard to attract the lucrative emigrant trade, which for many years was the income stream that drove their profits, and so standards were improving.

In second class, the food and service was of a far better standard; rather than long benches, it was served at tables in attractively appointed restaurants. By 1933, the Italian Line's *Rex* had four levels of dining: special, first, tourist (second class evolved into tourist during the mid-twentieth century), and third. All dining rooms and kitchens were on B-deck. A tourist dinner menu from 25 June shows five types of soup, chicken chasseur, glazed beef roundlet, a choice of vegetables, salads and sauces, desserts and coffee.

CUNARD LINE

R. M. S. "CAMPANIA".

THURSDAY, MARCH 17th, 1904.

. . BREAKFAST. . .

Oranges   Figs   Apples   Grape Fruit

Quaker Oats, Oatmeal Porridge, Boiled Semolina and Force Food
with Fresh Milk

HOT.

Fried Plaice

Broiled Finnan Haddie   Grilled Sprats

Fried Hominy Cakes—Maple Syrup

Eggs with Tomatoes to order

Grilled Cumberland Ham   Smoked Wiltshire Bacon

Omelettes to order   Eggs to order

Chipped and Mashed Potatoes

To Order from Grill—

Broiled Mutton Chops and Sirloin Steak

Mixed Grill to order

COLD.

Yorkshire Brawn   Capon   London Pressed Beef

Rolled Ox Tongue

Muffins   Griddle Cakes

White and Graham Rolls   Vienna Bread

Soda Scones   Scotch Oatcake

Watercress   Radishes

Tea—China, Green, Ceylon   Coffee   Cocoa   Preserves

RMS *Campania* breakfast menu, 17 March 1904.

First class could be more complex. On *Titanic*, one could dine in the first-class dining saloon, pay a premium to dine in the a la carte Ritz Restaurant, or dine in your parlour suite, if you could afford one.

Moving to the 1930s, the menu shown is for a special dinner on *Normandie* on 2 February 1938. It depicts the 20ft-high doors that gave access to this palace of gastronomy. The sheer scale of the choices – and the range of chefs, bakers, fish chefs, confectioners, sauce and soup chefs required to serve this level of cuisine – is incredible. The meal would have been served in *Normandie*'s stunning dining room, which was 305ft long, 46ft wide and 28ft high. This huge room had no external windows or portholes; it was entirely lit from within by glass-panelled walls with hammered glass inserts and concealed lighting, together with chandeliers and 16ft Lalique 'Fountains of Light' along each side of the room. If this wasn't exclusive enough, there were eight adjoining private dining rooms for more intimate gatherings. If you occupied a deluxe suite, dinner could be served in your own completely private dining room, or if you were more adventurous the café-grill offered fine food in a space that became a nightclub in the early hours.

On a modern liner such as *QM2* there is a huge choice of dining options. Many passengers dine in the 1,300-seat Britannia restaurant, a two-deck high, full-width room where two dinner sittings operate. There are also the Princess and Queens grill restaurants for passengers in premium classes, a self-service restaurant, steak restaurant and other options including The Golden Lion, an English pub. Afternoon tea is served along with midnight buffets or, of course, room service if you prefer.

Very few passengers have ever boarded an ocean liner with the aim of losing a few pounds!

43

WRITING HOME, LETTER CARD FROM TSS *GEELONG*

ON BOARD CORRESPONDENCE

In the days before telegraphic communication at sea, let alone email, the only way to let family and friends know that your ocean voyage had ended well, with safe arrival, was to write and let them know. Equally, the final letter posted on board before setting sail, an emotional farewell maybe or expressing excitement at the journey ahead, was a last link with home for weeks, or maybe years. Last letters of those embarking on a voyage, but soon to be lost at sea, are particularly poignant. Those sent from *Titanic*, posted perhaps at Queenstown, her last call before heading out in to the Atlantic, occasionally surface and sell for huge sums.

An ocean liner could carry the designation RMS, meaning Royal Mail Steamer. This meant that she was certified to carry mails under contract for the Royal Mail. Liners often had on-board sorting

... Lund's Blue Anchor Line ...

T.S.S. "GEELONG." 7,954 Tons.

J. E. ILBERY - - Commander.

Sydney, 4th Mar., Hobart, 7th Mar., Melbourne, 13th Mar., Adelaide, 18th Mar., 1908

(FOR CORRESPONDENCE.)

Dear ma— Sunday
Just arriving
in Adelaide - a beautiful
trip rain just splendid
Both boys. off Yesterday
a heavy. swell. Love
to self & Crichton from
all times for Hugh. A B L.

AGENTS.

WILLS, GILCHRIST & SANDERSON Ltd.,
Brisbane.
GILCHRIST, WATT & SANDERSON Ltd.,
7 Bent St., Sydney.
JOHN SANDERSON & Co.,
111 William St., Melbourne.
GEORGE WILLS & Co.,
Grenfell St., Adelaide & Fremantle.
WM. ANDERSON & Co., Capetown.
W. COTTS & Co., Durban.

HEAD OFFICE.

W. LUND & SONS,
5 East India Avenue, London, E.C.

LIST OF SALOON PASSENGERS

Mr. H. Allens	Miss A. Gellatly	Master J. Littleton	Mrs. J. B. Roe
Mrs. H. Allens	Mrs. E. Gillow	Master T. Littleton	Miss B. Roe
Mr. Astley	Mr. Gleeson	Mr. W. H. Lloyd	Miss M. Roe
Mr. S. G. Black	Mrs Gleeson	Mrs. W. H. Lloyd	Mr. K. P. Sawers
Mrs. Black and maids	Miss E. Hallam	Mr. H. G. P. Lloyd	Mr. F. J. Skipper
Miss C. T. Black	Miss H. Hewitt	Mr. N. D. Lloyd	Mrs. Skipper
Miss M. M. Black	Mrs. C. Hodgkinson	Mr. Pulteney Mein	Miss I. M. M. Skipper
Miss L. Bremner	Mrs. R. Honey	Mrs. Pulteney Mein	Miss E. F. Skipper
Mr. J Brothers	Mr. D. Honey	Mrs. Galbraith Moore	Mrs. Sleigh
Miss N. Oberlin Brown	Mr. C. Honey	Miss Galbraith Moore	Miss Sleigh
Mr. T. G. Cue	Miss Hoskins	Mrs. Henry Mort	Mr. E. R. Southhouse
Mrs. T. G. Cue	Mr. J Wallace Kidston	Master H. Notley	Right Rev. Dr. Stretch
Miss E Cue	Mr. E. Laroque	Mr. B. W. Pearse	Bishop of Newcastle
Mr. A. R. Dight	Miss Latter	Mrs. Pearse and child	Mr. E. C. Timbury
Miss L. Dolphin	Hon. E. Littleton	Mr. J. W. Rail	Mrs. J. Timbury
Mr W. W. Forwood	Hon. Mrs. Littleton	Mr. W. A. Rail	Mr. Oswald Watt
Mrs. Forwood	and maid	Miss M. Raye	Mrs. Oswald Watt
Miss M. E. Forwood	Miss J. Littleton	Miss E. M. Rice	and maids
Miss A. R. Forwood	Miss Y. Littleton	Mr. J. B. Roe	Master James Watt
Mrs. Gellatly			

	Chief Officer -	R. BIDWELL.	
Second Officer - - - -	C. OWEN	Chief Engineer - -	G. PEPPER, R.N.R
Third Officer - - - -	M. E. JAY	Surgeon - - - -	DR. M. SCOTT
Fourth Officer - -	J. ROGERSON	Chief Steward & Purser -	S. G. SKAILES

SS *Geelong* letter card.

On board correspondence from RMS *Saxonia* 1903.

offices that operated during the voyage. There was pressure to have the mails on shore at the destination ports as quickly as possible. Liners such as *Bremen* and *Europa* had mail planes that took off around a day out from port to deliver the mail to port well ahead of the ship. Many liners called at Plymouth in Devon on the way back from New York, as the mails could be offloaded and put on a fast train there to arrive in London or the north well before the ship reached Southampton.

Most liners had a writing room in first and, indeed, second class. This might have also served as a library with passengers able to borrow the latest books, to be returned by the last sea day. Writing paper and envelopes were provided, with the company crest and often the name of the vessel embossed. Postcards could also be purchased and posted en route in the case of voyages to the Far East or Australia. Las Palmas and Cape Town, Aden and Colombo were regular ports of call for these ships.

With the advent of wireless in the early 1900s, it became possible to communicate via Morse code over long distances and Marconi wireless operators worked from special on-board wireless offices, charging passengers, initially only the very wealthy, to send and receive business or personal messages. The operators on *Titanic*, Jack Phillips and Harold Bride, spent much of the voyage dealing with huge volumes of these messages, as well as trying to deal with operational messages, such as warnings of ice!

When the White Star Liner *Republic* was in collision in fog with SS *Florida* in January 1909 off Nantucket, her wireless operator, John Binns, became the first to send a CQD, which was the first internationally recognised radio distress code. Rescue ships came to the scene and only six people died in total from both ships. SS *Waratah*, which vanished later the same year off South Africa, had no wireless, although she doubtless would have had it fitted at some point had she not been lost.

The main image shows a letter card/passenger list from Blue Anchor Lines TSS *Geelong* from 1908. The captain shown is J.E. Ilbery, who was later to command, and be lost with, *Waratah*.

44

THE HALES TROPHY, SS *NORMANDIE* BLUE RIBAND CARD

CROSSING THE ATLANTIC AT SPEED, 1937

Since the early days of transatlantic travel, ship owners, passengers and interested observers ashore have been keenly aware of the prestige and publicity attached to the fastest liners to 'cross the pond'.

As we have seen, the race to build and operate the largest and most luxurious liners on the North Atlantic has been the subject of fierce competition between seagoing nations, and the issue of speed is no less so.

The issue of what constitutes a record is not straightforward. The westbound crossing was generally more demanding as a ship encounters the Gulf Stream, which it has to steam against to make progress. Fog off the Grand Banks could slow a record breaker, the award vanishing from sight as the ship had to slow down. This happened to RMS *Queen Mary* on her maiden voyage in May 1936.

Blue Riband card given to passengers on SS *Normandie* in 1937.

There were northerly tracks, which were taken from August to January, and longer southerly tracks, taken between January and August, when ice might be encountered further north. The start and end points might also vary. The transatlantic distance is around 3,000 miles. However, Queenstown (Ireland), to Sandy Hook (New York) might vary from 2,777 western northern track to 2,886 western southern. The run might be from Cherbourg, up to 3,164 miles, or from Bishop Rock to Ambrose Light, up to 2,971 miles.

The only way to find consensus is to take an average crossing speed. Here are some westbound milestones:

April 1838 *Sirius*. Queenstown to Sandy Hook,
   3,583 miles 18d 14h 22m, average 8.03 knots.
April 1843 *Great Western*. Liverpool to NY,
   3,068 miles 12d 18h 0m, av. 10.03 knots.
October 1876 *Britannic*. Queenstown to Sandy Hook,
   2,795 miles 7d 13h 11m av. 15.43 knots.
August 1891 *Teutonic*. Queenstown to Sandy Hook,
   2,778 miles 5d 16h 31m, av. 20.35 knots.
March 1898 *Kaiser Wilhelm der Grosse*. The Needles to Sandy Hook,
   3,120 miles, 5d 20h 0m, av. 22.42 knots.
October 1907 *Lusitania*. Queenstown to Sandy Hook,
   2,780 miles, 4d 19h 52m, av. 23.99 knots.
September 1909 *Mauretania*. Queenstown to Ambrose Light,
   2,784 miles, 4d 10h 51m, av. 26.06 knots.
July 1929 *Bremen*. Cherbourg to Ambrose Light,
   3,164 miles, 4d 17h 42m, av. 27.91 knots.
May 1935 *Normandie*. Bishop Rock to Ambrose Light,
   2,971 miles, 4d 3h 2m, av. 29.98 knots.
August 1936 *Queen Mary*. Bishop Rock to Ambrose Light,
   2,907 miles, 4d 0h 27m, av. 30.14 knots.
July 1952 SS *United States*. Bishop Rock to Ambrose Light,
   2,906 miles, 3d 12h 12m, av. 34.51 knots.

Close-up original photograph of The Hales Trophy.

SS *Normandie* officers and crew with The Hales Trophy on board, 1937.

The Hales Trophy was introduced in 1935 as an unofficial recognition of the fastest westbound crossing. Solid silver and 4ft tall, it was presented by British politician and ship owner Harold K. Hales. Only three liners actually received the trophy: *Rex*, 1935; *Normandie*, 1936; and *United States*, 1952.

Speed is no longer a feature of a transatlantic crossing. *Queen Mary 2* takes seven nights to cross, at a speed considerably less than her 30-knot maximum. The voyage is now the reason for the journey rather than the only way to cross, so why not relax and enjoy it? With her power plant, and were fuel economy not to be an issue, she could doubtless give the Blue Riband winners of the past a run for their money.

POSTED MISSING, SS *WARATAH* LETTER

COMPANY LETTER REGARDING MISSING PASSENGER SS *WARATAH*, 18 AUGUST 1909

After SS *Waratah* failed to make port, it was at first assumed that she had struggled with bad weather and would soon reappear. The weather conditions had in fact been awful at the time. Conditions off the Cape are influenced by the warm Agulhas current from the Indian Ocean meeting colder water coming up from the south, which, in combination with high winds, can produce extreme weather conditions. Waves of 20m have been recorded and many ships damaged or lost.

SS *Clan Macintyre* arrived in Cape Town to find that the faster *Waratah* was not there. SS *Guelph* reported exchanging signals with a ship on 27 July but could only make out the last letters of her name 'T A H'. SS *Harlow* reported seeing a large steamer in the distance

LUND'S BLUE ANCHOR LINE.

PASSENGER DEPARTMENT.

From

W. LUND & SONS,

5, EAST INDIA AVENUE,

LONDON, E.C., ___18th August___ 19_09_

Telegraphic Address: "Lund, London."
Telephone: 2414 London Wall.

To H. J. Roberts, Esq.,

Belliver,

Torquay.

In reply to your letter of yesterday, we do not know the Christian name of Mr. Stockem appearing on the Durban list of passengers per "Waratah" cabled to us by our Agents. We expect to receive on Saturday next, further particulars of the passengers who embarked at Durban according to the cabled list, and we will write you again.

Letter from Lund's Blue Anchor Line.

and two bright flashes like explosions. These were later dismissed as brush fires ashore.

So many possibilities. The search for the overdue *Waratah* would involve three Royal Navy cruisers and numerous other vessels. Ships traversing the area reported sighting bodies in the sea, one being a little girl in a red gown. In September the Blue Anchor Line chartered the Union Castle liner SS *Sabine*, which searched fruitlessly for three months, covering a large area well south of where *Waratah* was expected to be on the basis that she may have been disabled and drifted on the currents.

The ship was formally posted missing by Lloyd's of London in December 1909. In London, the inquiry into the loss of the ship began at Caxton Hall in December 1910. Experts, previous

Hand-painted 'Hands across the Sea' card, 1908.

passengers and crew who had sailed on her first voyage were called. Some said she was a comfortable ship that sailed well, others felt that she was top heavy and slow to recover from a roll. There was testimony that she had a permanent list.

What is certain is that she had vanished without trace. The court's conclusion was that she had capsized in a storm of extreme violence, so suddenly that most of the wreckage and bodies of those aboard were trapped within the hull and sank with her.

Mr Claude Sawyer, who unexpectedly left the ship at Durban, was not only alarmed by the ship's lack of stability. He had a recurring dream of an apparition clutching a sword and a blood-soaked rag. This seems to have saved his life, as his instincts told him not to continue the voyage.

The South African author and explorer Emlyn Brown has spent years searching for the ship and an expedition led by him found a likely wreck in July 1999, but it turned out to be a Second World War cargo ship carrying military hardware. The mystery has yet to be solved.

The letter shown is a poignant reminder of the human tragedy of SS *Waratah*. The Mr Stocken referred to was travelling with his wife and two children, aged 5 and 2. They were among the 211 souls lost, never to be seen again.

The loss of *Waratah* effectively put the Blue Anchor Line out of business, and their ships and routes were taken over by P&O in 1910.

AND THE WINNER IS ...,
ÎLE DE FRANCE TROPHY.

FRENCH LINE, 1930S AND '40S

On board a liner for an extended period, it is only natural that the passengers should look to the shipping line to provide a level of entertainment and diversion from what can be a monotonous daily routine.

On early liners, it was up to passengers, especially in steerage, to make their own entertainment. There were normally musically talented passengers with instruments aboard, or those with good voices and music might lead to dancing, while on a Sunday there would be hymn singing, possibly led by a clergyman, who were often aboard as passengers.

In first or second class, passengers would often form an entertainment committee at the beginning of the voyage. On the long haul to Australia, this responsibility and the success of the

SS *Île De France* silver trophy.

committee could make a voyage more than bearable. There was often a ship's newsletter to keep everyone abreast of planned activities and general notices from the captain and crew. On board SS *Waratah*, this was the *Waratah Prattler*.

On her maiden voyage the *Prattler*, dated 1 December 1908 and titled 'Off the South Coast of Africa', informs that the sports committee met in the forecastle on Monday morning and winners were announced for several events, including the boys' wheelbarrow race, the small girls' egg and spoon, and the ladies' collar and tie race, won by a Miss Williams. There is talk of a musical concert and the formation of a draughts league. Even interesting facts are included; did you know that 10,000 pieces of crockery were washed daily in the third-class pantry ... neither did I!

As time moved on, things became more organised, if not more sophisticated. In third class on *Berengaria* in June 1927, the itinerary takes in dancing on deck, a Charleston contest, pillow fights, a bridge drive and a beauty contest. *Normandie* in the 1930s offered trap shooting (clay pigeon) – luckily out over the ocean not across the lido deck! There were all manner of competitions, including a 'guess the daily distance' sweepstake, singing, bridge, sports and lotteries. There were dance competitions, fancy dress and children's entertainers and parties. On *Normandie* a notice advises of a boxing exhibition at 22.00 hours in the grand lounge, ending with a free for all against the 'confetti-weight of the *Normandie*'. This was followed by dancing in the grill lounge to the music of Bob Crislers.

Early liners might have had a band or small orchestra, but from the 1920s full orchestras would appear, as well as also dance bands and all manner of entertainers. There are clips online of Bunny Rowe and the Queen Mary Orchestra playing such memorable numbers as 'Fleet's in Port Again'. On a *Normandie* crossing on 22 November 1938, the Soiree de Gala featured Jack Warner as

MC and, among others, Gracie Fields accompanied on piano and singing 'Agnus Dei' and 'Ave Maria'. Afterwards, there was dancing to Georges Tharaud's Normandie Orchestra.

All a far cry from the Broadway-style shows, risqué comedians and cookery demonstrations you might find at sea today, but there are still competitions to take part in and prizes to be won, even if they aren't quite at the level of the gorgeous Christofle silver-plated trophies given away by the French Line in the 1930s and '40s.

SCRAPPING, RMS *OLYMPIC* MODEL

MODEL OF RMS *OLYMPIC* MADE FROM METAL RETRIEVED DURING HER SCRAPPING

All good things come to an end, ships being no exception. Liners that have had long, successful lives eventually become outdated, too expensive to run and maintain, or simply superfluous to requirement.

The model illustrated is made from metal salvaged from the scrapping of RMS *Olympic* by Thomas Ward & Co. of Inverkeithing, Scotland, and produced as a promotional souvenir. Launched on 20 October 1910, this sister to *Titanic* and *Britannic* was the only one of the trio to have a long and productive life. She had served as a troopship in the First World War, ramming and sinking the U-boat *U-103*.

Olympic, nicknamed 'Old Reliable', was finally withdrawn from service after twenty-five years, having started life as a coal burner

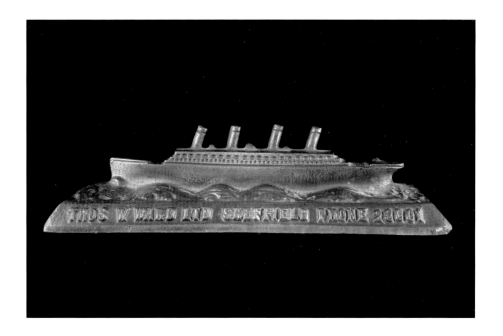

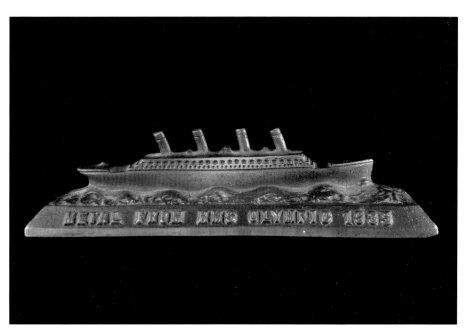

Model of RMS *Olympic* made from metal salvaged by Thos Ward & Co., Inverkeithing.

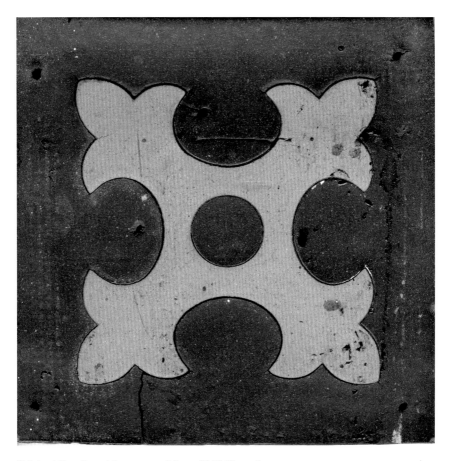

Original lino floor tile removed from RMS *Olympic*.

before being converted to oil in 1919. Initially laid up, her furniture and fittings were sold off. In October 1935 she went to Jarrow for partial demolition and removal of her superstructure and then towed on to Inverkeithing for final dismantling, which was completed by the end of 1937.

Dismantling was a labour-intensive, dangerous business. Ships were often run on shore at high tide on a foreshore that needed to be reasonably sheltered. Technology helped the process; a huge wrecking ball, hoisted aloft by steam power and dropped, could literally smash steel plates apart. Huge mechanical shears could slice through 2in steel plates. Oxygen-acetylene welding and cutting was developed at the start of the twentieth century and this revolutionised the shipbreaking industry. The downside for the workers was that two men could operate the new apparatus, replacing twenty-five men using the older methods.

Technology has, of course, moved on, but yet many of today's ships, be they liners, tankers, container ships or ferries, are broken up by hand on the beaches of Bangladesh, Pakistan and India. The beaches of Alang in the State of Gurajat on the Indian west coast are home to the largest shipbreaking enterprises in the world. There ships are run onto the beach at high tide. There are amazing videos on the internet showing vast tankers and container ships running ashore at high speed, and coming to a final halt high and dry on the mudflats. SS *Norway* (ex-*France* of CGT) was broken up here. SS *Canberra* of P&O suffered a similar fate in Pakistan, although she was too big to run ashore.

After beaching, workers will fix ladders to the ship and start to strip remaining fittings and dismantle it with torches and hammers. Some fittings and equipment will be recycled and sold on, while the rest will be reduced to scrap. Plates and parts are hauled ashore over the mudflats and further cut and broken ashore. The work is dangerous and there is a risk from hazardous chemicals, fuel, asbestos and other noxious materials. There is also a huge environmental impact.

Some pieces of historic liners remain. The White Swan Hotel in Alnwick is home to *Olympic*'s aft first-class staircase as well as panelling mirrors and restaurant doors. Linoleum tiles and other fixtures from *Olympic* were installed at the Haltwhistle paint factory in Northumberland and these periodically come up for sale.

48

CRUISING,
SS *NORMANDIE* BROCHURE

SS *NORMANDIE* CRUISE TO RIO BROCHURE 1939

A number of the liners discussed in this book supplemented their line voyages with forays into the world of cruising.

P&O possibly claims the title of the first dedicated cruise, when its liner *Iberia* toured the Mediterranean and over subsequent decades, many companies would follow suit. During the prohibition era, 'booze cruises' from the US became popular and, in addition to US ships such as *Leviathan* and *George Washington*, European liners such as *Mauretania*, *Berengaria*, *Rex* and *Normandie* would sail south to sunny West Indies or Caribbean climes for winter sunshine and quite possibly the consumption of large amounts of reasonably priced alcohol.

Some ships of this era were suited to cruising, with complete or partial air conditioning and ample lido deck space with pools

SS *Normandie* cruise to Rio brochure, 1939.

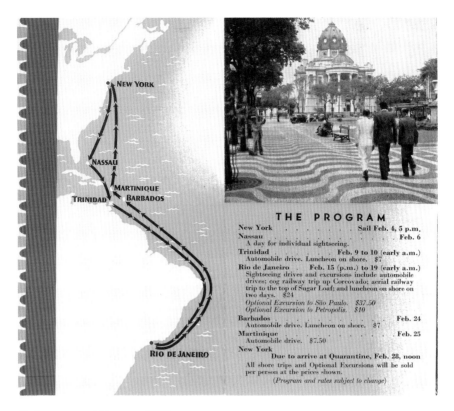

THE PROGRAM

New York . . . . Sail Feb. 4, 5 p.m.
Nassau . . . . Feb. 6
    A day for individual sightseeing.
Trinidad . . . . Feb. 9 to 10 (early a.m.)
    Automobile drive. Luncheon on shore. $7
Rio de Janeiro . . Feb. 15 (p.m.) to 19 (early a.m.)
    Sightseeing drives and excursions include automobile
    drives; cog railway trip up Corcovado; aerial railway
    trip to the top of Sugar Loaf; and luncheon on shore on
    two days. $24
    Optional Excursion to São Paulo. $37.50
    Optional Excursion to Petropolis. $10
Barbados . . . . Feb. 24
    Automobile drive. Luncheon on shore. $7
Martinique . . . . Feb. 25
    Automobile drive. $7.50
New York
          Due to arrive at Quarantine, Feb. 28, noon
    All shore trips and Optional Excursions will be sold
    per person at the prices shown.
        (*Program and rates subject to change*)

Cruise map and itinerary, 1939.

and recreational facilities. Others, such as the pre-First World War *Mauretania*, were not naturals in the role, but nevertheless, painted in white cruise livery, they went south. These cruises were often one-class affairs, and it was not until the late 1930s and post-war that liners specifically adaptable for this configuration were designed and built.

The first dedicated purpose-built one-class cruise liners can be attributed to the Nazis, of all people, and their 'Strength Through Joy' (*Kraft durch Freude*) liners. *Wilhelm Gustloff* and *Robert Ley*, 25,000 and 27,000 GRT, were extremely popular with German workers before the Second World War, while serving the Nazi regime as an excellent floating propaganda tool. Neither ship survived the war;

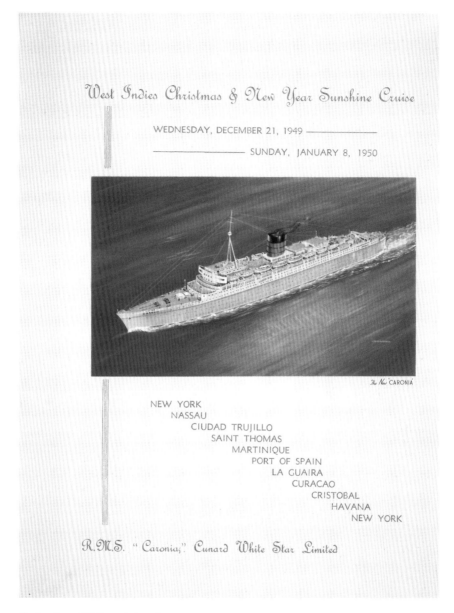

West Indies Christmas & New Year Sunshine Cruise

WEDNESDAY, DECEMBER 21, 1949 ───────────

─────────── SUNDAY, JANUARY 8, 1950

The New CARONIA

NEW YORK
NASSAU
CIUDAD TRUJILLO
SAINT THOMAS
MARTINIQUE
PORT OF SPAIN
LA GUAIRA
CURACAO
CRISTOBAL
HAVANA
NEW YORK

R.M.S. "Caronia," Cunard White Star Limited

Cruise liner MS *Caronia* brochure.

the *Gustloff* was torpedoed by a Russian submarine in the Baltic in January 1945. Nearly 10,000 people, civilians as well as German personnel and refugees, were lost, possibly the worst ever single loss of life at sea.

Cunard's *Caronia* was launched by HRH Princess Elizabeth on 30 October 1947. At 34,183 GRT, she was a one-class luxury ship designed for liner voyages, her first transatlantic one being in January 1949, and also to cruise. Painted in a distinctive livery, four shades of green, she soon became known as 'the Green Goddess'. She had art deco-inspired interiors and drew a huge following for her voyages, cruises and world cruises. Her funnel was painted in traditional Cunard red and black and was so huge that it acted as a sail which could make handling her, especially manoeuvring in port, extremely tricky.

Highly profitable, *Caronia* was finally withdrawn at the end of 1967 and sold on to a Panamanian company. Eventually renamed *Cariba*, she resumed cruising in 1969, but poor maintenance post-Cunard led to her being unreliable and she was sold for scrap in 1974. On tow to Taiwan, she went aground in a storm on the island of Guam, coming to rest on the breakwater of the port of Apra and blocking the harbour. She was cut up and removed, a sad end to a hugely popular liner.

49

ON-BOARD PUBLICATIONS, CUNARD MAGAZINE

CUNARD MAGAZINE, 1926

In your cabin, perhaps in a lounge or smoking room, or available from the purser's office – most liners offered some form of company magazine or periodical.

The main image shows the *Cunard Magazine* June and July 1926. Within its thirty-one pages are advertisements for John Brown & Co., Shipbuilders of Clydebank; along with Larranaga, the finest brand of Havana cigars; Horlicks; and the best place to buy your caviar, the world-renowned House of Benoist in Charing Cross Road.

Articles include 'Notes of a Nobody', a selection of snippets concerning Cunard goings on. These included news that *Mauretania* under Captain Rostron steamed 130 miles out of her way to help the disabled steamer *Laleham*, while *Ausonia*, 350 miles west of Bishop Rock, was able to provide provisions to the barque *Czaritza,* which had had her stores ruined in bad weather. Meanwhile the Great Western Railway was praised for a speedy boat train run between

Cover of *Cunard Magazine* June/July 1926.

Plymouth and London Paddington, a distance of 227 miles, in 230 minutes (including a two-minute stop near Newton Abbot!).

There is an article with pictures of happy passengers admiring the picturesque scenery of the Norwegian fjords from the deck of a Cunarder and a feature on the forthcoming Norwegian cruise by *Carinthia*: two weeks from Southampton, Oslo and the fjords and finishing in Liverpool. In other news, *Berengaria*'s deck department won the liner's challenge rowing cup, and recent passengers of note are pictured, namely Miss Dorothy Gish 'the well-known cinema actress' and Captain Roald Amundsen, the famous Arctic explorer. Mr Scott Skinner, known among fiddlers, as the 'Strathspey King' is also shown.

L'Atlantique was the daily on-board newspaper of the French Line and this special edition for *Normandie*'s maiden voyage has news-sheets inserted for the date, 11 June 1935, in both French and English. Advertisers include *Harper's Bazaar* of Madison Avenue, as well as Emile Genest, the 'Modern Detective' of Rue St Honare, Paris. Other advertisements include colonic irrigation by Aspiroclyse, Paris, and tango lessons by H. Roussel and Mme Balloy, the two being mercifully unconnected.

Articles include 'The Culinary Art of the Vikings' (fish and reindeer featuring heavily), 'Travelling in France', the history of Le Havre and quite a lot about French fashion. In the news, police captured the Weyerhaeuser Kidnappers, and *Normandie*'s captain, Rene Pugnet, announced that his ship had established a new east-bound record for a day's run from noon Saturday to noon Sunday, covering 711 miles at an average speed of 30.91 knots.

News could be sent daily by wireless, and thus passengers could keep abreast of world as well as shipboard events. Today, there will be a daily news sheet doing the same job, with a list of the day's events on board, as well as news and information about the journey. There is also access to the internet, satellite television and even a daily

Cover of French Line *L'Atlantique* magazine, *Normandie* maiden voyage (above) and an extract from *Cunard Magazine* (right).

Cunard Magazine

Recent Cunard Travellers.

(1) Miss Dorothy Gish, the well-known kinema actress. (2) Capt. Roald Amundsen, the famous Arctic explorer; and (3) Mr. Scott Skinner, known among fiddlers as the "Strathspey King."

216

on-board TV channel. There is no reason to be out of touch, but for many, myself included, the delight of an ocean voyage is to be able to forget the world and its worries during the days spent aboard.

50

BON VOYAGE, LINE-CROSSING CERTIFICATE

A *GRAF ZEPPELIN* CROSSING THE EQUATOR CERTIFICATE

All voyages have an ending. The end of the age of the great ocean liners was in many ways inevitable. The seeds were sown way back in 1927 when Charles Lindbergh made his historic New York to Paris flight, and in 1928, Dr Hugo Eckener's *Graf Zeppelin* airship began regular transatlantic crossings, firstly from Friedrichshafen to New Jersey, and later from Frankfurt to Rio de Janeiro. *Graf Zeppelin* made nearly 600 flights and carried 34,000 passengers in complete safety, many across the Atlantic. The end of the commercial airship came with the loss of *Hindenburg* in May 1937, and the beginning of the Second World War shortly afterwards.

A crossing the equator certificate given to a passenger on the airship *Graf Zeppelin* in 1936. Neptune does not look happy!

VIAJE DEL
Sr. MANUEL SOLA
EN EL "GRAF ZEPPELIN"
—1936—

Flying boats were another transatlantic option and Pan American began a service using huge Boeing 314 Clippers in 1939. The flights were not direct and had refuelling stops in Ireland and Newfoundland, but Germany was almost ready to start a nonstop service before the outbreak of war.

War tends to drive advances in technology, and the development of the jet engine by both Allies and Axis powers meant that by the early 1950s, the first jet airliner, the de Havilland Comet, entered service. By 1958 BOAC was running a transatlantic service using Comet 4s but it was the arrival of the Boeing 707 that was a game changer. In 1958 a Pan American 707 crossed from New York to Paris, via Gander, in eight hours forty-one minutes. From here, the road led to the 747, and Concorde.

On the Atlantic the liners carried on, but by 1963, 98 per cent of transatlantic travel was by air. The *Queens* were losing money for Cunard, and were known to run with more crew than passengers. By 1968, they had both been withdrawn. Liners were sent cruising to pay their way, but even Cunard's *Caronia*, a ship designed as a dual-purpose liner and cruise ship, was out of service by 1967. The Italian Liners *Rafaello* and *Michelangelo*, both built in the early 1960s, were gone by 1975. The huge SS *France* was withdrawn in 1974, but found a new life as the cruise ship SS *Norway* with NCL until 2008.

QE2 alone survived as an ocean liner. She entered service in 1969, well into the jet age, and was designed to replace the two previous *Queens*, retain Cunard's presence on the North Atlantic, and also to be a cruise ship. She was designed to be economical to run and could navigate both the Suez and Panama Canals, opening up ports denied to the older *Queens*. She remained in service until 2008.

Queen Mary 2 continues to run liner voyages and she is the last to do so. The massive cruise ships of today offer stupendous facilities, entertainment, dining options and levels of accommodation of which Eliza Putnam Heaton and Jack Thayer could have never dreamed. As we wave 'bon voyage' I hope that the objects and stories in this book have shown some of the links between past and present, and perhaps awakened the desire to set sail on new adventures.

Whimsical French card, two cats.

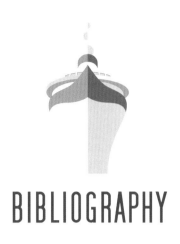

BIBLIOGRAPHY

Aylmer, Gerald, *RMS* Mauretania *The Ship & Her Record* (Percival Marshall & Co., 1934)

Ballard, Dr Robert D., *Exploring the* Lusitania (Weidenfield & Nicolson, 1995)

Britton, Andrew, *SS* United States (The History Press, 2012)

Broadley, Alexander, *The Ship Beautiful: Art and the Aquitania* (Cunard Steamship Co., 1914)

Kludas, Arnold, *Great Passenger Ships of the World* vols 1–6 (PSL, 1975–86)

Lord, Walter, *A Night to Remember* (Henry Holt & Co., 1955)

Maxtone-Graham, John, *Normandie* (Norton & Company, 2007)

Maxtone-Graham, John, *SS United States* (Norton & Company, 2014)

Miller, William H., *German Ocean Liners of the 20th Century* (PSL, 1988)

Miller, William H., *The Last Atlantic Liners* (Amberley, 2011)

The White Star Triple-Screw Atlantic Liners 'Olympic' *and* 'Titanic': *Souvenir Number of* 'The Shipbuilder', (The Shipbuilder Press, 1911)

Putnam Heaton, Eliza, *The Steerage: A Sham Emigrant's Journey to New York in 1888* (1919)

Rabson, Stephen & O'Donoghue, Kevin, *P&O: A Fleet History* (World Ship Society, 1989)

Sauder, Eric & Marschall, Ken, *RMS Lusitania, Triumph of the Edwardian Age* (Hallenbook, 1991)

Streater, Les, *RMS* Berengaria (The History Press, 2001)

Thayer, John. B., *The Sinking of the SS* Titanic (1940)

Williams, David L. and De Kerbrech, Richard P., *Cabin Class Rivals* (The History Press, 2015)

INDEX

Numbers in *italics* denote illustrations.

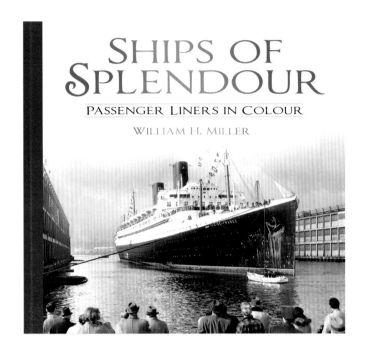